A LAND TO BELONG

NATIONALISM

SIMON LENNON

A Land to Belong: Nationalism
Non-fiction
Immigration
A book in the collection: The West
A book in the series: Nationalism
Published by Pine Hill Books
Copyright © 2016, 2021, 2023 by Simon Lennon.
All rights reserved.

ISBN 978-1-925446-05-0 (electronic)
ISBN 978-1-925446-17-3 (paperback)
52,000 words, plus bibliography, references to 56,000 words
Cover image: Cowra, 2012

In memory of my Great-Aunt Marjorie,
of Ashfield

CONTENTS

1. THE NEED FOR COUNTRY

A word we use to describe the West unilaterally opening our borders to all is globalisation, but it isn't globalisation. It's individualism. The West dreams of a world without nations, globalism, but when we give up our countries, we don't gain the world. We just lose our countries.

Our only rights to land (and everything else) are as individuals. We might own pockets of soil, if that, or spaces of air.

Outside the West, we don't even have that. With our single-world view, we're the citizens of the world, but the rest of the world doesn't recognise the concept. Globalisation is countries trading and otherwise relating with each other, with citizens aware of what's happening elsewhere.

Most countries outside the West have opened windows to the world. All of them retain their walls. Openness is for their peoples, not everyone else.

Openness is for their peoples, not everyone else; a multiracial world doesn't require multiracial countries. Foreigners can visit, perhaps stay and work for a while, even a long while or for the rest of their lives, if those countries have no reason to reject us. Those countries revoke foreigners' permission to remain if their people's interests require it.

Racially homogenous countries aren't closed societies. They're simply societies, serving people within them rather than people wanting to enter. Their lands are theirs, not anyone else's. With the comfort countries are and all that countries give them, their lands are distinct and, to the extent they can make them, inviolable. Their globalisation rests upon their nations, not ours, bettering their peoples while, for the most part, leaving each other be.

Fifty countries adopted the United Nations charter in June 1945: the month after World War II finished in Europe and while it remained under way in Asia and the Pacific. "*The Purposes of the United Nations are,*" begins article 1, before the second paragraph says, "*To develop friendly relations among nations based on respect for the*

principle of equal rights and self-determination of peoples…"
Self-determination of peoples is nationalism. The United Nations charter assumed relations between nations: internationalism. Nationalism isn't a matter of superiority, but equality.

A country is a people with territory, but we're no longer peoples. For all our rights in our postmodern West, a rare right we don't have is a right to a country: a land to belong. Our view of institutions like the United Nations progressed from being means of nations interrelating to structures superseding nations altogether. We might be the smallest of minorities or, for the time being at least, the majority, but our nations aren't changing because we have no nations to change. What were a myriad of countries throughout Europe, North America, and Australasia became the near-seamless West.

We used to consider ourselves to have racial rights to territories, with the comfort countries were and all that they gave us. Other races still do. Why wouldn't they? Human nature is to want a home. The most natural feeling on earth is for people to own the lands of their birth, even if we no longer do, while identifying with their ancestral lands, which we no longer do either. For indigenous peoples, those lands are one in the same. For everyone else, they're not.

Colonial Europe's descendants pay great heed to the races we call indigenous and their need to link with their land, according them collective ownership to defined areas now unimaginable for us. Since 1974, New Zealanders have celebrated as a national holiday each anniversary of the signing of the Treaty of Waitangi between the Maoris and the British on the sixth day of February, 1840. The Americas are awash with Native American homelands, according tribespeople rights within and without. Europeans in our new homes allow them something of their countries we don't consider for us.

When we British settled in Australia in 1788, naked Aborigines carrying spears and sticks had left the land almost completely untouched. The continent was the most primitive place we'd seen (Antarctica remaining undiscovered until 1820). Nevertheless, the Australian High Court in 1992 handed down judgment in what quickly became known as the *Mabo* case, rejecting the traditional view that Australia had been *terra nullius*, nobody's land, in 1788. It initiated a process formalising Aboriginal tribal rights to land: native title.

In 2012, the Arabana people were granted title over seventy thousand hectares of the South Australian outback, including Lake Eyre. Arabana chairman Aaron Stewart explained that "our land is identity, it's who we are."

We could say the same for white people, but no longer do. Without land, we lack identity, definition: something to ground us. Without a country, what have we? We have nothing.

In 2013, sixteen thousand Aborigines owned ninety-seven thousand square kilometres of Arnhem Land, which other Australians could only enter with permits from the Northern Land Council. Local Aborigines allowed Bruce to visit because the former Ku-ring-gai municipal councillor came to help them. The right we respect for other races, we don't claim for us.

The Aboriginal and Torres Strait Islander Act 2005 established the Indigenous Land Corporation to help indigenous people acquire and manage land to achieve social, cultural, economic, and environmental benefits, exempting it from anti-discrimination laws. The most natural thing in the world for the new Aboriginal owners of Yulara, a Central Australian tourist resort, in 2011 was to increase employment of their fellow Aborigines among the six hundred and seventy strong workforce. The discrimination we'd condemn in our treatment of foreigners is all well and good when practiced by indigenous peoples against us.

"Let me begin," say the hosts and hostesses introducing school presentation nights, concerts in parks, university debates, and other public gatherings in Australia, "by acknowledging and respecting the traditional owners and custodians of the land, their elders past and present." A school captain said it at our local primary school although he was Persian, speaking as he was told to speak. We smile warmly each time a child expresses the custom of our era.

Those revered owners and custodians are normally named. They used to be us. They're now Aborigines who came before us, specified by the particular tribe. In the case of our local municipality, it's the Guringai.

By November 2013, our local primary school letterhead included the statement, below the school name and addresses: *"Built on the land of the Guringai people."*

The first words that viewers of my eldest son's high school

website saw were that the school was *"in Guringai Country. We acknowledge the Guringai People as Traditional Custodians of the land and pay our respects to Elders past and present."*

By August 2015, the high school administrative manager's signature to her electronic mail didn't begin with her name. Instead, *"I acknowledge the traditional owners on whose land I work, the Guringai People."*

I've never met any Guringai people. I doubt any of the speech-makers and scribes have. They might be extinct.

Indigenous tribes don't need to exist for us to recognise their links to the land. In 2008, Hornsby Shire Council issued its Statement of Reconciliation with Aborigines. *"The land we now know as Hornsby Shire is home to the spirit of many generations of the Darug and Guringai peoples."*

Those introductions and recognitions are the norm in Australia, declaring the land to be Aboriginal, disenfranchising us from the country. They would have been certain to be repeated at an official dinner in the Great Hall of Sydney University in September 2012.

Completed in 1859 when Western architecture exuded our race and civilisation, the Great Hall was a mammoth Victorian Gothic stone structure modelled upon Westminster Hall, London. Barrister Jeffrey Phillips, Senior Counsel, began his address by acknowledging the "traditional custodians of this place." Instead of proceeding to speak of an Aboriginal tribe, he spoke of the "Benedictines who came from the great English nation."

One indigenous student lodged a formal complaint with the university. She was said to be "deeply traumatised."

"How disgusting," said Mark Spinks, chairman of the Aboriginal men's group Babana, "how disgraceful, how disrespectful are those comments? I am outraged, and I am disturbed. For that to have been said at the university, in a room full of students, I am almost speechless."

Spinks wasn't actually speechless. He was almost speechless.

We were just as outraged. "It's just an indication of how deep the rot goes," said sociologist Eva Cox. Phillips was senior counsel of the university's prestigious St John's College, which had been the subject of scandal of late.

"The university is very proud of the fact that it stands on land where indigenous peoples have been teaching and learning for many thousands of years before us," said vice chancellor Michael

Spence, "and we acknowledge this publicly whenever we can."

We revere Aborigines for what we think they did on the land, although there's little or no evidence of what that was. They left no grandiose great buildings, not even branches leaning against tree trunks, but they're the people we've decided could have remained wonderful, their societies glorious, if only we hadn't come.

Immigrants aren't generic. They weren't simply immigrants but British who built Australia and New Zealand centuries ago. French built Quebec and Louisiana. British built the rest of Canada. British, Germans, and other North Europeans built most of America. Portuguese built Brazil. Spanish and other South Europeans built most of the rest of Latin America. Other Europeans contributed, depending upon colonial powers employing or allowing them. Europeans built countries in and away from Europe, before and after other races came. We contributed to countries we didn't build.

We whose forebears sailed from Europe to build our mother empires no longer feel the lands to which we were born are ours. Time and again, we declare them other people's lands. Indigenous people agree.

There was no sense of one-world openness to immigration when Sydney City Council removed all reference to European "*arrival*" from its official documents in 2011. The word was unacceptably neutral, when we wanted prejudice against us. "*In 1788,*" said the new Aboriginal and Torres Strait Islander Statement, "*the British established a convict outpost on the shores of Sydney Harbour. This had far reaching and devastating impact on the Eora Nation, including the occupation and appropriation of traditional lands. Despite the destructive impact of this invasion Aboriginal culture endured and is now globally recognised as one of the world's oldest cultures.*"

We see much merit in something being old, unless it's ours. We don't care that our forebears came without meaning to harm. We deride them for thinking they could do any good.

When colonial Europeans first arrived, indigenous peoples didn't feel invaded. Without nation states, tribes staked out no more than valleys, watering holes, and so forth; nomadic tribes didn't even do that. Europeans setting camps nearby didn't affect them, especially when they presumed Europeans were passing through. Conflicts arose when they both wanted the same land, as they did between indigenous tribes.

If colonial Europeans owe such copious regret to the indigenous peoples whose lands we entered, then the immigrants we graciously allowed to come owe us gratitude. As it turns out, they don't. We owe them apologies for not admitting them sooner.

The same week that Sydney City Council decided Europeans colonising Australia were invaders, Australian Chinese demanded an apology from the Australian government for, among other things, past immigration policies preventing Chinese from immigrating en masse. "The time has come for a number of Chinese Australians to get rid of the last vestiges of white superiority," declared Daphne Lowe Kelley, president of the Chinese Heritage Association of Australia.

With no sense of appreciation but only complaint, what she really wanted was another tranche of white inferiority. No one cared that the Chinese government refused to offer citizenship to people of other races born in Hong Kong when it took control of the British colony in 1997. No one considered apologies from Chinese and other governments that still aren't admitting immigrants as we now do. We're completely uninterested in restrictions other races impose upon immigration.

Instead, we're preoccupied with restrictions we used to impose. New Zealand, Canadian, and Californian governments had already apologised to their Chinese immigrants.

We think refusing other races immigration into our countries makes them our victims. We don't imagine ourselves victims of them denying us admission to theirs. The only nations we reject are our own.

So consumed are we with what we can do for other races, we insist immigrants and their successive generations feel greater rights to be in colonial European countries than we allow ourselves. Borders we refuse to recognise to keep other races immigrating to the West stand stark in the sky when we remember our colonial period. Ignoring borders here in the present, we imagine borders that weren't there in the past.

We denounce our forebears for entering other peoples' homelands uninvited, not complying with laws where there were no laws with which to comply, breaching borders where there were no borders to breach. We damn them still further for keeping other immigrants in check.

Indigenous peoples didn't give up their homelands as we give up ours, as they often remind us and we often recall. We respect them fighting our colonial forebears in defence of their land, presuming they're right to deny us a welcome we'd be wrong to deny anyone else. Their rights to prevent us coming weren't rights we had to prevent other races coming.

We accommodate other races more generously than they accommodate each other. We accommodate them more generously than they accommodate us.

Fa'a Samoa, the Samoan way of life, includes cultural traditions such as communal living and a belief that the islands' lands should stay in Samoan family hands. "Basically, what it comes down to is freedom — the freedom to own communal land," said Filipo Ilaoa in 2020. Most property in American Samoa is owned communally among families.

The land "ties you back to your family name," explained Bonnelley Pa'uulu, acting director of the American Samoa government's office in Hawaii, "and it's like where you belong." She planned eventually to return to American Samoa.

Rights to land ownership are often not simply restricted by citizenship. They are restricted by race.

By 2020, more than three times as many American Samoans lived in the Continental United States than lived in American Samoa. That was no reason for American Samoans to let Americans buy land there. Samoan law restricts the sale of most property to anyone with less than half Samoan ancestry.

Similarly, the Commonwealth of the Northern Mariana Islands requires land owners to carry at least a quarter Northern Marianas blood. The Northern Marianas is an American territory that grants American birthright citizenship, but American courts have upheld the Northern Marianas blood requirement for land ownership.

The West thinks little of countries, at least our own, but if we really believed all peoples are the same, in some primeval instinctive ways, we'd see in ourselves what we respect in others: our yearning for a collective connection to country. We would want countries and a continent as other races want or enjoy.

If we are not so bold as to dream of recovering our countries and continent completely, we can at least stop our circumstances worsening. We could only accept immigrants from countries that accept the same immigrants from us: bilateral immigration.

We could stop beckoning people to come with jobs our

compatriots could do, welfare benefits, or anything else. We could prohibit trespass.

We could do what the rest of the world does. Instead of granting foreigners rights to reside in our countries, we might grant them permission to stay. Their permission might be nominally permanent, through the rest of their lives, but always with the caveat we can withdraw that permission if our compatriots' and national interest require it. Our compatriots' interest is our national interest. That is nationalism.

Foreigners can be tourists, students, executives, or workers, along with their families, but their holidays, studies, or jobs would not be at our compatriots' expense. We would pay foreigners wages and salaries for work they performed, but not welfare or pensions. We would not pay or subsidise the costs of their healthcare, children's education, or anything else. Aside perhaps from a few specific categories of resident applicants or noteworthy individuals, we would not offer foreigners or their children citizenship.

The permission we grant, we would grant only the good. From the bad or possibly bad, we would revoke their permission to stay.

We do not expect other races to sacrifice or suffer for our benefit. Why must our compatriots and descendants sacrifice or suffer for their benefit?

Generous as we are, we might grant our friends refuge, but only refuge and only for as long as they need it. If people visit our home and forever sit in our sofas, eat from our kitchens, and sleep in our beds, generation after generation, then it is no longer our home.

Wanting a country to own isn't fear or loathing, prejudice or bigotry. It's not for American Indians, Australian Aborigines, or New Zealand Maoris whose craving for their homelands we so wildly applaud, or for Asians we admire. Nor is it for Palestinian Arabs we support or Israeli Jews we defend. It's not for Africans to whom we send money or Turkic peoples we leave be. Nor is it for Tibetans for whom we place stickers on our cars, or Uighurs and Kurds whose killers we shelter.

We can like all the people and places on earth, but still need countries of some kind. Other races don't insult us by not letting us live in their lands. We wouldn't insult them if we did the same.

If we honoured our ancestors as we honour other races' ancestors, we'd respect not just our indigenous hosts. We'd respect our forebears who created our countries inviting to others, many dying to defend them.

Instead, we're a string of ideologies by which we advance other races at the expense of our own. We're immersed in self-sacrifice: deferring to everyone else, demanding nothing in return. If we landed on the lunar surface today, we'd begin by acknowledging the traditional owners of the moon.

2. A EUROPEAN HOME

If our land to belong can't be the land in which we were born, then it's the land from which our forebears sailed. If Australia is the Aboriginal ancestral homeland, then Britain is my ancestral homeland. Europe is Europeans' ancestral land, whether we live there or not.

The Sunday afternoon after Australia Day 2008, I drove my three eldest young children past the comfortable houses near the Australian War Memorial, finding our way. (It's never too hard to find our way in the middle of Canberra.) Standing in the centre of an otherwise quiet intersection was an Aboriginal woman, with crazy, grey hair and a tortured face. Her shaking stagger and endless chatter without an audience reeked of drug and alcohol abuse, meaning we'd make several excuses for everything she did. When our car approached, she stepped into our path and screamed, "Get out!"

Unlikely to have lived in the pretty street she guarded, she seemed to scream for the country no longer hers. We feel our indigenous people's anger for what they say they lost when we came, accepting them demanding we leave our colonial homes as we would not accept our race evicting anyone, not even from Europe. They're free to hate immigrant us, while we welcome subsequent immigrants.

As I drove around her, she contorted her body and hurled her fullest indigenous spit towards us. No white person screamed as she screamed, or spat as she spat.

I was momentarily furious with her, as she was already furious with us, but our furies didn't matter. No one was hurt, no damage done. Her spit didn't reach our car.

She remained in the centre of that intersection behind us, ready to confront every other car coming as she'd confronted ours. I telephoned the police not to report a crime, but for someone to keep her from injuring herself or somebody else.

There's no reason for colonial Europeans to leave, unless other immigrants go too. They can care for their ancestral homelands, knowing those homelands care about them more than anyone else beyond their borders. Most of them have choice where they live between the disappearing West and those homelands in which they belong, wherever they happen to be. We don't.

Among the endless Western stories marketing immigration was one by journalist Paola Totaro in 2010. As is customary, she reduced Europe to an economy enjoyed by the rich paying low wages, assumed work done by immigrants would be left undone without them, ignored poor Europeans condemned to welfare, and dismissed crime and the economic detriment due to immigration as mere accusations. What bothered Totaro was the electoral success of political parties concerned about immigration amidst economic recession and governments adopting austerity measures saving two hundred billion euros. *"The notion of xenophobia-driven politics is nothing new to Europe. But the economic crisis has created a new tension that is seeing post-war pledges never to repeat the horrors of the past thrown out the window in the scramble to win votes."*

I wondered when we could finally let go of the war that ended sixty-five years earlier: World War II. None of our touting diminishes the real reasons the West accepts immigrants from all races: fundamentally, because it's against our national interests. We think our national interest means not having nations, believing nations led us to war. Without collective identities, there can be no collective conflict, no countries to combat. We don't want nations anymore.

Globalism is our overarching desperation to avoid conflict, however much people suffer. We could have kept our countries without malice on our part, learning not to fight each other, but we yearn to lose and lose without learning anything. We head straight to defeat.

John Monks, the general secretary of the European Trade Union Confederation in Brussels, feared economic problems returning racism and nationalism to Europe. He insisted that people remember the 1930s as if they'd been bad times with our racism and nationalism, but recovering from the Great Depression and away from Soviet communism, most European life pre-war was good.

Monks wasn't thinking about Europeans. "…Europe has been successful in respecting the rights of minorities in past decades," he said, without consideration of when Europeans would be minorities. "There are localised problems, yes, but I never cease to be agreeably surprised at the relaxed reaction of most people. Just look at the changing face of London."

We have no choice, but to seem relaxed. Otherwise, people would hate us.

"I had a Californian friend come over two months ago," said English comedian John Cleese of London 2011, "walk down the King's Road, and say to me, 'Well, where are all the English people?' I love having different cultures around but when the parent culture kind of dissipates, you're left thinking, 'What's going on?'"

Cleese's experience could have been replicated in any number of Western cities, but any white person not wholeheartedly embracing immigration provokes controversy. Only a month or so after the English riots, mayor Boris Johnson (whose great-grandfathers included a Moscow Jew and a Muslim Turk) insisted London's racial diversity should be celebrated. (It shouldn't be questioned.)

"To stay competitive London must be a global centre of business, culture, and innovation," claimed former mayor Ken Livingstone, "none of which can be achieved without people of all nations working and living here." His were the words of a race no longer confident in itself. Asian and Middle Eastern cities don't feel the need for immigration to stay competitive, even if they permit particular foreigners to live and work there.

Besides, Cleese's point was that people of all nations weren't working and living in the King's Road. English people weren't. While we weep for other races being subsumed, we welcome other races subsuming us. We're the willing white minorities, becoming strangers in the lands of our birth. Our sense of a single planet supersedes Western streets, suburbs, and countries: a planet without us.

"*I'm an American of English descent and I've had more trouble entering the UK than any other country,*" commented Kensmith on the *Sun* newspaper website. "*Here is just one example. Several years ago, I was traveling from Nice, France to Aarhus, Denmark, changing planes at Luton. I arrived on an easyJet flight, then had to go through immigration because the RyanAir flight was at another section of the airport. Even though I showed my departure ticket to the immigration officers, a Polish woman and a Sikh man,*"

I was asked where I would be staying in the UK and the purpose of my trip. I tried to explain that I would be in the UK only a few minutes. I needed to walk across the airport to catch my next flight.

"The Sikh man said little, but the Polish woman, seeing my US passport, told me she was once made to wait four hours when entering the US at Philadelphia. Then, she told me I might be held because the photo on my passport was slightly "delaminated".

"Then, in frustration, I asked about a right of return. I told the officers that my grandfather as a young boy a century ago had herded dairy cows right where we were standing, before the Luton airport was built. I added that my direct paternal ancestors had lived in Oakley, Bedfordshire, for at least 300 years.

"The Polish woman was not impressed by my roots. Finally, she did let me pass and I barely had enough time to catch the flight to Denmark."

Colonial sons and daughters visit our ancestral lands as foreigners, confined to long queues at airports, ferry terminals, and railway stations. Hurried ahead of us are people whose passports make them European, as we're deemed not to be. (Western countries discriminate on the basis of passports.) We're the homeless colonials, Mother Europe's bastard children, who don't belong there anymore. Our mother countries abandoned us, while we ran away.

Cleese said his words in an Australian television interview, but I found no mention of it in Australian newspapers. Instead, I found a story about Samoan footballer Manu Tuilagi, introduced *"From illegal immigrant to the next Sonny Bill."* Sonny Bill Williams was a Samoan playing rugby league in Australia. *"While Tuilagi is now seen as the future of England rugby, just over a year ago the government wanted to deport him after it emerged he had arrived in the country as a 13-year-old on a six-month holiday visa and since stayed on illegally. Leicester considered letting him play for Samoa and bringing him back as an overseas player. But Tuilagi wanted to play for England and British authorities eventually gave him special dispensation to stay."*

England rugby's future wasn't simply immigrants. It was illegal immigrants.

Without Europe to call ours, neither can Europeans in Europe: the ones who never left. There, we're the indigenous peoples, but indigenous identity is selective: an eminence we don't offer ourselves. We're the only races to whom we don't recognise indigenous rights. Those of us who remained get no particular recognition, no special status in their ancient homes. No host or hostess begins a gathering at the King's Road, London, by acknowledging and respecting the traditional owners and custodians of the land, their elders past and present: the English.

We define Europe with all the races in residence. Anything else would be racist.

If we become a little bit envious of our friends from immigrant races, then it's because they have ancestral homelands, back home across Asia, Africa, and the oceans. Moving around the world, they can hark to their homes behind them they might never see. They needn't live there to know their countries, races, and cultures endure. The borderless West can collapse and Koreans in Kentucky know Korea is safe. Most of those homelands are racially homogenous. Those that aren't leave no doubt that their ancient peoples predominate.

Sometimes, far from the eyes and ears of the mob, we try to breathe a little. My father, stepmother, and stepsister lived in a medieval villa overlooking Florence through 1997, where my stepsister immersed herself in the land of her father. My father knew an African-born woman struggling to get legal permission to live in Italy, until she appeared at the relevant government office. The officials were surprised to see her, having presumed she was black. Away from the laws and rules prohibiting racism in everything we think, feel, and do, officials quietly approved residency for a woman courteous and white.

Their racism harmed no one. It aided at least one. It aided Europe. If the officials hadn't been racist, they might still have refused her request to remain in Italy before meeting her, but would have continued refusing her request when they did.

"What do we mean by discrimination?" Quintin McGarel Hogg asked Britain's House of Commons in 1968, advocating the Commonwealth Immigrants Bill granting people who'd left Britain a limited right of return. "I do not believe that it is racial discrimination in any offensive sense if one says to people in that relation to oneself that we recognise some special and residual obligation towards them when they come to our own country. It is not offensive to take this attitude. Any other would not be realistic. I object to duality of standards. If the Lebanese can do it to the Lebanese who return from Brazil, we are entitled to do it to people who have this kind of relation with us. I do not see anything offensive in it."

Europe's rights of return are matters of law. They're rights to live and work in places without presumption our hearts are there.

The British right to return, such as it is, vests only in the children and grandchildren of British citizens. "This is not a racial bill," Hogg had been careful to say, as had the government of the day. Being British is no longer racial, but national. Thus my late brother-in-law Bill and his wife, the younger of my sisters, could live and work in the land of his grandparents. There's no racial entitlement as would make my wife or me eligible.

Europe could respond to her low birth rates by allowing all her treasured offspring to return: to be as welcoming of our prodigal peoples as we've become of everyone else. We would again be her sons and daughters, returning home to repopulate, any number of generations after we left to populate our colonies. We'd be ancestral Europeans in our ancient lands, if our ancient lands allow us.

Africa for the Africans was a theme through our withdrawal from Africa following World War II (although it hasn't kept Africans from killing each other since then). If we should leave our lands of empire because they're not our ancestral lands, then other races should leave Europe. If European races don't belong outside Europe, then other races don't belong in Europe; Europe for Europeans.

If our past imperialism condemns the Americas and Australasia to being multiracial elsewhere, then it needn't condemn Europe. For those of us remaining in our colonies, the conflicts and crises of multiculturalism would be easier to bear with our ancestral homes and heritage intact, our future secure, as they are for immigrants. We could be at the far side of the earth never touching lush European soil, but not fret so much for the New World we're losing.

British writer Arthur Clarke's novel *2010: Odyssey Two* was first published in 1982. At the time, European peoples led on the one hand by America and on the other by Russia and her Soviet Union were fighting an ideological conflict between ourselves: the Cold War. Escalation into hot war across the Iron Curtain dividing us could have killed tens of millions, again annihilating Europe. Asian countries were rising, at our behest.

In the novel and film, set in a future 2010, a mathematically neat, black monolith orbited the planet Jupiter. A joint American and Soviet mission investigated the causes of the disaster described in Clarke's earlier story *The Sentinel* written in 1948 and the 1968 film derived from it, *2001: A Space Odyssey*. In *2010*, a Chinese spacecraft seeking water landed on Jupiter's sixth moon, Europa, where an indigenous life form killed the Chinese crew.

Sitting in a Sydney cinema with my girlfriend in 1985, I'm not sure when I first perceived the film in terms of the planet Europa being the continent Europe. By the time the American Hal-9000 computer interpreted the message transmitted by the monolith, the metaphor was unmistakeable. *"All these worlds are yours, except Europa. Attempt no landing there. Use them together. Use them in peace."*

I first drafted this text with the year 2010 little more than a year away, the Soviet Union long disbanded. I'm revising it three, four, five, and then six years after 2010 passed, without monoliths appearing in space. We survived the Cold War, but only after East Germans and East Europeans suffered and died under communism.

Fundamental to the Soviet failure was its pursuit of a multicultural globalism denying peoples their nations. Globalism means eradicating countries, their borders and identities, as the Soviet Union and then the West set about doing.

The motherlands Europe once shared with her faraway children, she revoked. She can revoke what she's offered the rest.

Normally people pay a price for a country, but immigrants enjoy residence in our lands because we gave it to them. What we've given, we can recover. We've come to disavow notionally democratic governments when they embark upon wars with which we disagree, turn away immigrants we would admit, or expel people we'd allow to remain. We could just as easily disavow them for having admitted immigrants, rescinding those immigrants' permission to stay.

Ours would be discrimination with courtesy, in favour of our own. Without Europeans in Europe, we're not anywhere, while gypsy strangers take our place in the Pyrenees.

3. RACE AND COUNTRY

Western globalisation used to be predicated upon nations, spreading civilisation to improve people's lives and make the world better. That was imperialism. The education we provided Bennelong taught him to write a letter late in August 1796: the first by an Australian Aborigine.

Also among the National Library treasures on exhibition in June 2023 was a notice of Aboriginal protests on Australia Day, 1938. We did not yield before World War II as we yielded afterwards. Weakened by a second world war and without faith anymore in the civilisation we'd spread, the age of European empire ended in 1945.

Where we'd entered other races' homelands, we withdrew, coming home to Europe, America, and Australasia. The United Nations called it decolonisation, removing Europeans from Africa, Asia, and the Pacific (but not Asians from Africa or the Pacific). Tribes and races across Asia, Africa, and the oceans became again nations they'd once been and countries they'd never before been.

Something else happened, because our end of empires wasn't about empires. It was about us. Self-determination for races is racism. Without it, we lost our resolve to occupy not only other people's lands, but ours too. Respecting rights for other races, left to their countries and choices, we lost notions of nation for us. We lost our senses of race, and soon lost our senses of home.

Our rejection of race is our rejection of country, no matter how many other races are among our citizenry. Anything else would be discriminatory.

Interracial immigration, in significant numbers, depends upon the decline of our racial identities. Nations make little sense without race. Nationalism makes little sense without racism. Geographical delineations make little sense without biological delineations. Without being a people, we can't be a country.

A race can comprise many nations. A nation ultimately comprises only one race.

Uniquely in the world and through history, the West freely gave up our racially homogenous communities. Races from whom we'd kept apart, we admitted into our homelands, suburbs, and streets. Our gates opened wider and wider; our arms were opened to all. Nobody invaded. They came because we allowed them. What's become the most dramatic demographic change of all time was voluntary.

Through holiday and work, I've often visited Europe. My first day in London was Armistice Day 1979, a Sunday, sixty-one years after the Great War ended. Sometime after the parades had passed and poppies set to rest, my father and I came across scores of angry Africans and South Asians marching in mob unison. Without our reason for remembrance, they'd usurped the streets, obstructing the paths of passers-by. Police mustered people with white complexions to the footpaths to wait, while the marchers' banners and if memory serves me well, their voices, defiantly shouted: "*We are here because you were there.*"

They claimed that British colonisation of Africa, the West Indies, and South Asia necessarily led to them being in Britain. It didn't. Races all over the world conquered each other without them thinking that conquest invited the conquered into the lands of their conquerors.

Descendants of peoples the Mongol Empire conquered and colonised with mixed-race offspring aren't making their way to Ulan Bator. Japan's colonial possessions aren't colonising Japan.

Africans and South Asians were in Britain because British governments let them or their parents come. Still they protested the discrimination they said they suffered.

While my father and I watched that march on one part of London, English people in another part of London protested the loss of their country to immigrants. The two competing demonstrations slowly and deliberately marched towards each other. "We should just leave them to each other," a policeman said to my father and me, but no one's more polite than the British police. They kept the two marches apart.

Non sequitur refers to concepts with no logical connection that people nevertheless link. During my last visit to Dublin, in 1998, an Irishman in the street insisted Ireland should allow more immigrants because other countries had accepted Irish émigrés, but the countries accepting Irish émigrés weren't the countries offering émigrés he wanted Ireland to accept.

Most, perhaps all, races have moved around the globe, to the extent they could. In recent years, that's been primarily to the West. Longer ago, the more entrepreneurial races enjoyed the opportunities European empires provided to pursue wealth for themselves. Without thought of spreading civilisation, Chinese, Indians, and others became prospectors, shopkeepers, and traders across most continents and oceans, even a little in Europe. For the most part, they stayed. We think our past emigration requires us to accept immigration. Other races don't think the same of their emigration.

In August 2007, while evading arrest for illegally selling music and film discs, Nigerian criminal Tony Onouha jumped or fell from a first-floor cafeteria window in Thessalonica, igniting four days of rioting by Nigerians (and some Greeks) across Greece. "The tragic death of the young man from Nigeria reminds us all of the difficult days we Greeks experienced a few decades ago, when we emigrated to make a living," responded Thessalonian prefect Panayiotis Psomiadis. "It is the duty of the Greek state, whose development was influenced by emigration, to show sensitivity and attribute blame where necessary."

Sending émigrés didn't just oblige Greece to accept immigrants, but to be sensitive to them. I wasn't sure if Psomiadis was saying that Greece should relax her intellectual property laws to accommodate immigrants, or Greek police should simply not enforce them against immigrants. Greece's émigrés never rioted in their destination countries as Nigerians rioted in Greece.

(Without Psomiadis' words, I might never have known the dead man or most rioters were Nigerian. I didn't recall seeing media reports about them at the time, but more than a year later stumbled upon them because of subsequent riots in December 2008; reports of both riots simply mentioned them being Greek. The only published photographs of the latter were of white rioters, although they might have been a year earlier too.)

Countries discriminate if they offer something, however little, more to their citizens than others. The French government should have known better when it sought to promote French culture among young citizens of the European Union in 2009. The benefit was so meagre as free entry to the Louvre Museum, but still *S.O.S. Racisme* complained that the offer was discriminatory. Our countries came to exist for the benefit of people within no more than without.

The last day of April 2009, I returned to Sydney University for the opening of the new law school building. By then, student union and representative council election campaigns were far more resourced than they'd been when I studied there, more than two decades earlier. When first I saw a woman alighting at Redfern railway station wearing a tee shirt campaigning that someone should be on the union board, I assumed it was a trade union, but I proceeded to the university awash with people wearing similar tee shirts. If the people wearing them didn't pay for them, other people did.

Student union election posters weren't just on noticeboards but on the dark timber walls and steep rows of desks in the John Woolley Building lecture theatre, where I'm sure I'd sat in lectures. The posters were the only things obviously new since I'd last been there.

One poster, partly covered by other posters, on a noticeboard was for Kate, a candidate for Student Representative Council president. I'd have pushed the other posters aside to see her surname if I could, but they were all behind glass. (If someone with a key hadn't put the posters there, then someone else had slipped them between the glass panels. I couldn't slip them any further.) On Kate's poster was her website address, www.Kate4prez.com, perhaps with a suffix hidden behind another poster. (Later, from my home, I tried to access the site, but it was inoperative. Perhaps her poster was from a past election.)

Kate's poster was interesting because she didn't talk of bicycles and rickshaws as other candidates did. (Really, they did.) Her first of a few reasons why people should vote for her was to get *"An SRC that campaigns against racism and all forms of discrimination,"* presumably part of her campaign to change the council and the country.

As best as I could tell from the monochrome photograph on the visible part of the poster, Kate was white. Not only did she want to eliminate all forms of discrimination, she focused upon racism above all else: the worst of all wrongs. Other candidates weren't so focused as she was, distracted as they were by bicycles and rickshaws.

Kate wanted international students to enjoy the public transport concession fares enjoyed by local students. She had no sense that the fares were a treat subsidised by other passengers, or that Australians who weren't students didn't receive them. Discrimination by student status was fine, discrimination by citizenship was not. She was standing in a student election, after all.

Such a frenzy do we have around national discrimination, a Dutch shareholder was furious to read a 2010 Australian prospectus offering shares only to shareholders with registered addresses in Australia and New Zealand. The restriction was customary because offering shares in other countries would have required Golden Cross Resources Limited to investigate and comply with laws in those countries, but that was hardly the point.

"Just red your prospectus," he wrote, and spelt. (His English-language spelling was better than my Dutch-language spelling, or would have been, if I knew any Dutch.) *"As a shareholder with a registered addres in The Netherlands, I am excluded from the issue of new shares. And that is putting it mildly as you could easily call it discrimination and make that stick. Discrimination is forbidden in all civilized countries and that includes yours."* (Presumably all those countries outside the West where discrimination is the norm aren't civilised.) *"Hence the Prospectus is unlawful and a respectable company like ours unworthy and I demand that the restriction towards foreign shareholders is stricken from the Prospectus.*

"Thank you for your attention to this unacceptable issue. Best regards..."

In fact, he held his shares through a nominee with an Australian registered address so could subscribe, although that can't have diminished his fury. Nor could it have helped that Australian law compelled the company to appoint a local nominee to buy and sell the shares of ineligible shareholders remitting any net proceeds to them. Foreigners fared better.

Discrimination against foreigners we meet with abuse, even if the discrimination isn't to their detriment or our benefit. 'Picking on the foreigners,' was the heading to one gem of a news article late in 2010 by Richard Farmer. He wasn't writing about anything so mundane as train fares or share purchases. *"Xenophobia is taking a new form in the Netherlands. The country's Justice Minister Ivo Opstelten said yesterday that in the future, only residents of Dutch cities will be allowed to purchase cannabis. 'Not tourists. We don't like that,' he said.... The Opstelten proposal marks another step back from the liberal policies of Dutch tradition."*

Being a recent tradition didn't matter; our contempt for

tradition isn't for our new liberal traditions. Purchasing cannabis remained illegal in other countries, which I imagined allowing drug tourists to claim refugee status in the Netherlands.

Fundamentally, the West welcomes immigrants because we reject racism. It follows that our compatriots wanting to limit immigration are racist. A draft paper drawn up for the British Home Office in 2000 acknowledged the British people wanted more restrictions on immigration, but dismissed it because *"anti-immigrant sentiment is closely correlated with racism."* Far from acceding to public opinion in what was nominally a democratic country, the paper wanted ministers to change that opinion; we don't accede to racists. The government sought large increases in immigration to meet its *"economic and social objectives."*

Those points were censored from the paper published the following year: another official endorsement of the supposed economic benefits of immigration, without mention of popular opposition. In the ten years before the draft paper became public information, Andrew Neather, a former adviser to Prime Minister Tony Blair and ministers Jack Straw and David Blunkett, revealed the government's *"driving political purpose: that mass immigration was the way that the Government was going to make the UK truly multi-cultural."* The government secretly wanted to change Britain and, divided as we are by politics, *"rub the Right's nose in diversity."*

Pursuing multiculturalism through immigration, we aren't blind to race. We want other races: a rush of new arrivals.

"In 2004," admitted former cabinet minister Lord Peter Mandelson in 2013, "...we were not only welcoming people to come into this country to work, we were sending out search parties for people and encouraging them, in some cases, to take up work in this country." Mandelson went onto admit, "We have to just realise... entry to the labour market of many people of non-British origin is hard for people who are finding it very difficult to find jobs, who find it hard to keep jobs."

The political purpose of mass immigration could have also been votes. In our post-national democracies, immigrants vote for more of their people's immigration.

For the sake of their votes, Australian governments after the election of 1972 allowed immigrants to bring in their relatives. *"Governments since then,"* wrote Richard Farmer in 2010, *"have been too scared to abandon family reunion as a significant method of determining the migrant intake for fear of losing votes from what has become a corner stone of the Australian version of multiculturalism.*"

Academic and former ambassador Stephen Fitzgerald's report *Immigration: A Commitment to Australia* to the federal government in 1988 found major problems with migrant selection mechanisms, widespread community mistrust of the immigration programme, and the undervaluing of citizenship. It recommended examination of Australia's economic and social interests in the course of developing immigration policy and that social harmony be a key consideration.

The report was filed away. Votes from other races mattered too much.

If Western countries retain any role, it's to work against racism. We vet people not for race, as other countries do, but racism. Not ours, but theirs.

American Michael Savage, born Michael Weiner, graduated from college with a bachelor's degree in biology, two master's degrees in ethno-botany and anthropology, and a doctorate in nutritional ethno-medicine in Fiji. Ethno-botany appears to examine the relationships between plants and different cultures. Ethno-medicine seems to study medical practices that aren't Western in origin. None of those courses I recall being available when I set out on my tertiary studies.

Those disciplines linked race with something other than race. In 1994, publishers rejected Savage's manuscript *Immigrants and Epidemics* for being insensitive.

Whether his manuscript was true didn't matter. It was insensitive.

Savage became a radio commentator, calling the Koran a "book of hate." He would later say his words were quoted out of context. He wanted the American government to stop illegal immigration and urged Americans to burn Mexican flags. The Paul Revere Society he headed "stands for the reassertion of our borders, our language, and our traditional culture." Among his statements for which he later apologised was calling autistic children "brats" in need of discipline.

Savage opposed violence but from October 2008, the British Home Office banned him from entering the United Kingdom, and not because the British hadn't forgiven Paul Revere. Ironically, I'd never heard of Savage, Weiner, ethno-botany, ethno-medicine, or ethno-anything else until the Home Office banned him. Savage was Jewish.

What made Savage a particularly good choice for banning was his condemnation of homosexuality. *"I think we could be accused of duplicity in naming him,"* acknowledged one British civil servant (a rather paradoxical title in the circumstances), before adding that *"the fact that he is homophobic does help."*

The ban put Savage in interesting company. In May 2009, the British Home Office advised that the sixteen people it banned also included Hamas parliamentarian Yunis Al-Astal, Jewish extremist Mike Guzovsky, two leaders of a violent Russian skinhead gang, the former Ku Klux Klan grand wizard Stephen Black, and neo-Nazi Erich Gliebe. I'd never heard of them either, until they were banned.

Multiracial immigration doesn't reflect love for immigrants. It reflects scorn for white people.

English comedian Bill Oddie became famous in the 1970s as one the Goodies. In 2014, Oddie didn't just want more immigration to Britain. He wanted restrictions upon the size of British families, to prevent over-population. "I'm happy to say I'm not proud to be British," he said. "In fact, I'm very often ashamed to be British. We are a terrible race, all the hooliganism and God knows what."

It might have been that the British people he really hated were the working classes. For that, he hated his race.

Oddie disregarded most British behaviour. He disregarded immigrants' behaviour altogether.

White people wanting our countries back don't hate other races. We just don't hate our own.

4. THE ZIONIST PARADOX

At one of my old school friend gatherings, my half-Lebanese friend Mark exhorted immigration. We've had a few conversations about immigration in Chatswood, where the Chinese are so predominant, although they're less prominent in the Great Northern Hotel than elsewhere. In response, I asked Mark something along the lines: "If immigration's so great, why doesn't Japan have it, or China?"

Mark fell silent. He'd never thought about that.

We talk of the narrowness of nationalism, but when we abandoned our empires and opened our nations to all races, we became oblivious to everyone else. So self-centric have we become, we don't think much beyond our close social boundaries. We think even less of the far side of the world. We see immigrant faces in our country, feel they flatter us by coming, and believe they're like us. Ours is a one-world ideology, without regard to the rest of the world.

The most striking verification for the failings of immigration comes not from the countries that embraced it as from those that haven't. We might have imagined them following our lead, giving up their people and countries into a big global pot. Seventy years after we began, they're still not buying into it. Our great gesture hasn't moved them to take the course we've taken; it just hasn't happened. Not a single country outside the West has opened its borders as we have. The few countries there incurring immigration, as we understand it, restrict it to their race or, into Israel, religion.

In ancient times, conquests of Judah scattered the Jews. They became the first global people.

Immersed so much in his work, American Jew Bryan Singer directed some very fine films. An adoptee as a child and bisexual, he described alienation and feelings of not belonging (evidenced in his 2006 film *Superman Returns*) as universal themes, but they're not. They're postmodern themes as much for Jews as Europeans. He saw themes of discrimination in his 2000 film *X-Men*, which others saw in the comics upon which the film was based. The film opened with scenes of Jewish prisoners during the Holocaust.

Since World War II, Jews and we have followed two primary strategies in our determination to avert another Jewish Holocaust. The first is eradicating white racism.

To that end, we have immigration. Argentina is the only Latin American country currently with net immigration. Argentina also has the largest Jewish community in Latin America.

Amidst the furore after Collingwood Football Club president Eddie McGuire suggested Aboriginal footballer Adam Goodes promote the musical *King Kong* in 2013, journalist Sam de Brito suggested Australia remained racist because, unlike America, there weren't enough black people around to attack white racists. "*Even the dumbest, most rusted-on American racist knows if you call a black person a nigger, you better bring it, because you're gonna get a savage reaction...*"

Mixing with a handful of people from other races might make us sympathetic or antagonistic towards them. We need a lot of them to be afraid.

Besides, with so many other races around us, we're less focused upon Jews. Anyone aspiring to cleanse our countries of other races has so many races through which to work, the Jews are unlikely to be the first to go.

The second strategy is to create a place where Jews are safe. That isn't just the Florida retirement villages. It's a nation for Jews: the state of Israel.

The two strategies are contradictory. It's absurd to reject the concept of race while maintaining there should be, or even could be, a racially Jewish state, but we do.

By electronic mail, my French friend Patrick, a chef, periodically informed his friends of important anniversaries of Napoleonic campaigns with accounts so detailed that, were he not so diligent a student of history, I'd have assumed Patrick fought in them. If not loading the muskets, he'd have been making the cakes.

A proud Frenchman, Patrick described the Dreyfus Affair as among the greatest stains on French history. Napoleon attacking Austrians, Prussians, and Russians didn't bother Patrick as did the wrongful conviction for treason of a single French Jew, Captain Alfred Dreyfus, in 1894. Ironically, given events three decades later, Dreyfus was accused of being a spy for Germany.

I don't know if Patrick's message came before or after I borrowed the 1937 American film *The Life of Émile Zola* from a local library, but the affair that meant so much to Patrick made less of an impression on me. While Dreyfus' initial conviction seems to have been an error, events two years later made the affair notorious. In 1896, evidence pointed to Major Ferdinand Esterhazy being the spy, but French military officers used false documents to exonerate Esterhazy and further implicate Dreyfus.

Through the ensuing years, French society polarised between Dreyfus' defenders and detractors. Dreyfus was brought back from the Devil's Island penal colony in French Guiana in 1899, tried again, and ultimately exonerated. In 1906, he was restored to the rank of major in the French Army.

Sixty years later, my friend Patrick was born. A hundred years later, the Dreyfus Affair still shamed him.

Dreyfus' most vocal supporter, the atheist writer Émile Zola, wasn't Jewish, but Theodor Herzl and other Jews believed they could only be assured of justice in a Jewish country. Zionism is Jewish self-determination: a Jewish homeland. The Zionist movement preceded the Dreyfus Affair, but the affair was its biggest impetus until the Holocaust. Modern Israel came into being in 1948.

Jews became less global. Open borders disempowering dominant races are for our global West, but not fortress Israel. It has accepted Ethiopian and other Jews not racially Jewish, along with other refugees, but the numbers are tiny aside Western admissions. They're huge only in comparison with other countries outside the West.

The inconsistency was most evident during the Camp David negotiations between Israel and the Palestinian Arabs in 2000. No other Israeli government had offered more in pursuit of peace, but among the few irreconcilable issues was a Palestinian right of return like that for Jews. The seven hundred thousand Arabs who'd fled during the 1967 Six-Day War had grown to four million, but Israel offered to allow only small numbers to return for humanitarian and family reasons, along with monetary compensation. Four million Arab immigrants would end the Jewish state not by war but democracy. Negotiations failed.

Israel's parliament, the Knesset, enacted the Law of Return in 1950 and Nationality Law in 1952. The former declared Israel the natural home of Jews the world over, irrespective of whether they or their known relatives were Israeli citizens. A 1970 amendment to the Law of Return extended the Jews' right to return to Israel to their spouses, children, and grandchildren, as well as their spouse's children and grandchildren.

There are limits. The Law of Return allows Israel to deny Jews citizenship if they're dangerous.

Individual Jews might have never before set foot in Israel, but the right to return is a racial return to the land their ancestors left thousands of years earlier. Israel doesn't deny Jews entry for being atheists, although the 1950 Law of Return excludes Jews who voluntarily adopt a different religion. In April 2008, the Supreme Court of Israel acknowledged that Jews who hadn't been religiously Jewish couldn't renounce Judaism. They could return.

Also entitled to live in Israel are converts to Judaism, although Jews debate what makes a person a convert to Judaism. Simply choosing to become a Jew, as another person might choose to become a Christian, isn't enough.

Israel allows other foreigners to live and work in Israel without offering them citizenship. Babies born in Israel can only get Israeli citizenship if at least one parent is a citizen. Non-Jewish permanent residents may only obtain citizenship after at least three years living in Israel, renouncing previous citizenships, and demonstrating their knowledge of Hebrew. Israel will not cease being Jewish because of immigration.

In the seven years after 2005, sixty thousand Africans escaped poverty and persecution by entering Israel, where many committed rapes and other crimes. Without Western tolerance but an assertion of statehood we no longer imagine, Prime Minister Benjamin Netanyahu said, in 2012, that the influx was "threatening the fabric of Israeli society, its national security, and its national identity." If Israel failed to stop them, he said "sixty thousand infiltrators are liable to become six hundred thousand, and lead to the eradication of Israel as a Jewish and democratic state." If he'd been white, he'd have been a xenophobe.

Netanyahu also held the health portfolio. A year later, in 2013, Israel admitted that gynaecologists had been administering the birth control drug Depo-Provera to Jewish Ethiopian immigrants without their knowledge or consent, after journalist Gal Gabbay investigated the sudden fall in their birth rates. "They told us they are inoculations," said one Ethiopian of the medical staff. "We took it every three months. We said we didn't want to."

The public revelation stopped the practice. The Ministry of Health told doctors *"not to renew prescriptions for Depo Provera for women of Ethiopian origin if for any reason there is concern that they might not understand the ramifications of the treatment."*

Higher birth rates of immigrant races in the West than ours don't bother us. Higher birth rates for Ethiopians than Jews in Israel bothered some Jews. Higher birth rates for Arabs in Israel bother Jews more.

Former American president Jimmy Carter spoke in January 2009 of the three options Israel faced to remain a Jewish state in the face of its changing demographics. Firstly, Jews could disenfranchise its burgeoning Arab population, much as white South Africa did with its black majority, but the numbers eventually become so overwhelming as to make majority rule inevitable. Secondly, Israel could expel the Arabs. Thirdly, Israel could partition its territory so that Israel becomes a slowly shrinking state, which was the only option Carter considered when he espoused the creation of another Arab state: Palestine.

In our postmodern hierarchy of people, we defer to other races because we think they're all victims of us. We aren't sure who to choose when they're at odds with each other.

Jews built Israel from the sand and defend it from growing millions of Arabs and other Muslims wanting them gone. Arabs have more rights in Israel than in most Arab states, but Palestinian Arabs complain about democratically elected Jews rather than life in a land under Arab authority.

Much as white South Africans ceased being able to rely on support from white people outside South Africa through the twentieth century, so eventually did Jews. Increasingly, we lumped Jews with us in refusing them their self-determination; a thousand years and more in Europe had failed to do that.

Having removed Western borders, we're upset that Israel believes in its borders. Other countries outside the West also enforce their borders, but they don't have millions of Arabs on their doorsteps wanting to enter.

Having decided to welcome everyone, eagerly becoming minorities in what were our cities and countries, we think Israel should too. We have no sympathy for Israel not also welcoming a Muslim majority. Arabs become victims of Jewish defence.

Disenfranchising Jews from the West would be unacceptable

anti-Semitism. Disenfranchising them from Israel is more acceptable anti-Semitism; they too can all come to the West. Opposing self-determination for Jews in the land they have often occupied through millennia while supporting Palestinian Arabs wanting that land, with so many states already Arab, can only be anti-Semitic. Anti-Zionism is socially acceptable anti-Semitism.

Europeans (other than Germans) frown upon Jewish Israel as we would never frown upon Jewish Antwerp. In our darker moments, we blame the loss of our countries upon Jews.

Muslims aren't so divided. At the 2001 World Conference against Racism in Durban, South Africa, Muslim countries labelled Israel as racist. No country cast that label upon Muslim countries, but anti-Semitism, anti-Christianism, and anti-anything else don't constitute racism for Muslims the way defying Muslim hegemony in the Middle East does.

The West doesn't equate Zionism with racism; we think only white people are racist. Muslims equate Zionism with racism, and they're right, but across Africa, Asia, and the oceans are other racial states at least as racist. A hundred million Arabs and other Muslims aren't complaining about them.

Palestinians aren't planning to accommodate minority Jews in their state as Israel has accommodated them, or as the West accommodates both. "After the experience of the last forty-four years, of military occupation and all the conflict and friction," said the Palestinian Liberation Organisation ambassador to America, Maen Areikat, in 2011, "I think it will be in the best interest that the two peoples should be separated."

He did contemplate they might eventually change their minds, but with another looming United Nations vote on the issue of a Palestinian state, that he said anything was surprising. "I think we can contemplate these issues in the future." That future was after the eradication of Israel.

Orthodox Jews reject the notion of a Jewish state, Israel, until the messiah comes. Wanting segregation without statehood, Orthodox Jews retain well-defined communities, separate from everyone else. Racial integration isn't always a Jewish vision, not even in the West.

The Holocaust didn't destroy the faiths of all Jews. For the Orthodox, it affirmed it. They see the *Shoah* as God's punishment for Jews having started to integrate with Gentiles in the decades beforehand.

The Holocaust that gave Jews their land to belong ultimately cost white people ours. We surrendered our senses of belonging because we didn't want anything separating us from the Jews; our countries became homes for them as much as for us. We have to be able to share neighbourhoods with other races, we think, because we have to be able to share the world with them. To question whether different cultures can share a city is to question whether different races can. It's not an issue outside the West, where countries remain.

God gave the Jews Israel. He didn't give them the West.

Racial and religious tolerance doesn't require indiscriminate immigration. "*We believe in religious and racial tolerance among our citizens*," declared the fifteenth statement of Liberal Beliefs issued by Australia's Prime Minister Robert Menzies and Liberal Party federal president William Anderson in 1954. The White Australia Policy restricting immigration to white people and Jews remained.

While hailing our liberalism and democracy, we've become increasingly uninterested in reflecting the wills of white people on matters of race since the Holocaust. We might have majority white populations, but don't deny other races their rights to come and to grow. We'd punish anyone suggesting we should, but if we responded to birth rates among the Orthodox Jews in Borough Park, Brooklyn the way that some Jews responded to them among Ethiopians in Israel, there'd be lots of inoculations in Brooklyn.

5. THE REST OF THE WORLD

"I think Europe belongs to the Europeans," said the Dalai Lama in 2018. He was in Malmö, Sweden, with a large immigrant population.

The Tibetan leader had fled Tibet in 1959, fearing for his life after a failed revolt led to Chinese troops pouring into his country. China had occupied Tibet since 1951.

Perhaps for that reason, the Dalai Lama believed Europe was "morally responsible" for helping "a refugee really facing danger against their life," (unlike people the West accepted as refugees by 2018), but only while that danger continued. "Receive them, help them, educate them...but ultimately they should develop their own country." The wars they'd fled having passed, refugees should return home as "they ultimately should rebuild their own country."

In 1959, India granted the Dalai Lama refuge on that basis. There, he led a government in exile.

Races other than ours enjoy governments defending them. They want countries.

Siti Chamsinah was among the Indonesian nationalists detained by the Dutch during World War II. With the Japanese invasion, the Dutch wanted the detainees transferred to Australia, where Chamsinah spent half a year detained in Cowra before studying nursing in Melbourne. Talking about it sixty years later, she said the Australians treated her and other Indonesians well (although I dare say that won't deter us from apologising to them).

"I didn't feel like helping Dutch soldiers because they had invaded my country," she said in 2008. The Dutch withdrew from Indonesia in 1949. "The training came in handy later for my own people."

By her own people, she meant Javanese. Chamsinah helped her race.

We don't help ours, but in a quixotic effort towards a multiracial nationalism, we tried to save from execution in Indonesia drug smugglers Andrew Chan and Myuran Sukumaran because they were Australian citizens. They'd not felt Australian nationalism when they led a group of nine citizens trying to smuggle dangerous drugs to Australia in 2005.

Indonesia prepared to execute them, while saving more than sixty of its citizens from death sentences in China, Iran, Malaysia, and Saudi Arabia, according to an Amnesty International report in 2012. Only we in the West complained at Indonesia's double standards. Of course, they were double standards: the double standards governments apply standing by their people.

They favour their people wanting to prosper, ahead of others wanting prosperity. They retain what they have by discriminating against others. Their people protect them.

In the 1970s or so, an engineer friend of my father was working in the oil-rich Middle East when an Arab crashed his car into the rear of the car the engineer was driving. In the West, the Arab would've been responsible for the crash; road rules oblige drivers to keep their cars far enough behind the cars ahead of them to ensure they can stop without driving into the back of them. In the Middle East, an Arab driving the rear vehicle would've been held responsible if he'd crashed into the rear of a car driven by another Arab, but the Arab policeman held the foreign engineer responsible for the collision. "He wouldn't have crashed into you if you weren't in the country," he explained.

It was all perfectly logical. When countries outside the West allow people to come, it's in their national interests. They might be impoverished but want money. They might be wealthy and see value in the work foreigners do that their people can't, or won't. They allow tourists and workers, without imagining we're anything else. Theirs is a right to defend their kin and themselves: expelling those who'd harm their countries, cultures, and compatriots.

The United Arab Emirates is among the richest countries on earth. Emiratis aren't willing to work the lowly paid jobs that foreigners are. They lack the skills of Western expatriates providing expertise. Foreigners leave Dubai when their work is done. They can't obtain citizenship or vote, although Dubai forbids political parties and allows only limited elections and democracy anyway. The laws governing local people aren't being changed to accommodate others. Police prosecute foreign men flagrantly drinking alcohol and foreign women conspicuously wearing bikinis on the beach.

Emiratis nevertheless valued something in their lives they lost with foreigners numbering more than ninety percent of the population in 2008. "Everybody who lives in this country," said political scientist Abdel-Khaleq Abdullah about Dubai, "whether they are citizens or expats, can sense how massively difficult it is to be a minority in your own country and feel such pressure on your habits, your language, your religion. We are at the point where we need to talk about this frankly. We feel that our identity and all its components are under threat... The fundamentals of the entire growth model need to be rethought to fit our demographic needs."

Immigrants amount to such proportions in parts of the West, are often unemployed, and are staying for generations upon generations, but we insist we're lucky to have them. Similar remarks by a white person about our changing circumstances would have attracted outrage.

By the standards of the world, we're strikingly nice, far and away the kindest and most welcoming peoples on earth, but aren't so racist as to imagine us being nicer than anyone else. Others know we are.

For many years, Libyan leader Muammar Gaddafi made much of opening Libya to black Africa in his condemnation of past European colonialism, but it was all big-people politics. Ordinary Libyans referred to black Africans as "*abid*," meaning slave or servant, as Kenneth Ansu discovered entering Libya from Ghana in 2008. "I thought the people would be white and that white people were kind," he said in 2011. "Ha, ha, ha! What a fool."

I was surprised to read Libyans being lumped with Europeans among a generic white people, but Ansu no longer made that mistake. "Libyans are bad people," he said. "They don't respect humanity. They let their children throw stones at you and say nothing. They beat you in the market with impunity. They cover their noses when you get on the bus."

The West's unilateral niceness entices people to come without thought of complying with our laws. "With the strength of God," continued Ansu, "I will struggle to find a way to Europe. Perhaps save a deposit for a visa and then overstay, but never Libya or the desert."

Africans and other races took up our sense of a West without borders, while keeping their countries. Although fewer have returned to Africa in recent years, African Americans have been colonising the region now called Liberia since 1820. Becoming citizens as people born there of other races cannot, the Liberian Constitution restricts citizenship to black Africans.

More sensible than we are, they think of themselves. They care for their compatriots, ancestors, and descendants. They're not letting their landscapes become multiracial as they're making ours.

Modern Olympic Games tend to celebrate there being one world. Outside the West, that's a world of nations. For the extravagant opening ceremony at the 2008 games in Beijing, performers from the Galaxy Children's Art Troupe dressed in distinctive costumes. Gleefully they paraded through the stadium, representing China's fifty-five minority groups, but the children were all Han Chinese: multiculturalism without multiracialism.

East Asians value homogeneity and conformity, not merely for being Confucian. My Hong Kong Chinese friend Ted champions multiculturalism, but only for Australia. China remains China: pure and secure.

Do Han Chinese on the island of Taiwan acknowledge indigenous Taiwanese as the traditional owners they displaced? Do they in Tibet?

Nor are we espousing diversity there. We want countries outside the West to tolerate minority races already present, but don't expect them to allow immigration. Thinking that countries without us would be better for our immigration was our past colonialism.

South Koreans have a word pronounced "*Dan-il minjok gook ga*" to describe their single-race society. While we insist immigration and racial diversity bring economic benefits, the Central Intelligence Agency's *World Factbook* in 2010 said South Koreans believe racial homogeneity empowers their economic development.

Nationalism isn't isolationist, narrow, or conservative. In 2011, Australian National University scholar Emma Campbell saw Korean racism developing a "global cultural nationalism." In their interpretation of "our nation, *uri nara*," young South Koreans take pride in the modernity of their society, technologies, and global corporations. Valuing education, international values, and speaking foreign languages, they accept the few foreigners living there speaking Korean (who don't get citizenship or other rights Western counties give Koreans) as well as American Koreans.

Believing West Germans had incurred too much cost to reunify with East Germany in 1991, Campbell thought younger South Koreans would be less welcoming than their parents of the backward North Koreans imprisoned into ignorance behind communism since 1948. I mentioned her view to a man who'd spent time in Korea, who thought Koreans wanted their race and country unified again. For all the nuttiness the Northerners suffered, they're Koreans. Nationalism is ultimately racial, and the South will welcome a reunified Korea modelled upon the South. North Koreans wouldn't be immigrants, but Koreans on Korean land.

Outside the West, governments and even brutal dictatorships at least claim to defend and advance their people's interests. The North's objective is a reunified Korea modelled upon the North, which is why Korea remains divided. The North-South Declaration of the fifteenth day of June 2000 left no doubt as to the only race involved. *"The South and the North have agreed to resolve the question of reunification independently and through the joint efforts of the Korean people, who are the masters of the country."*

Dictatorships like those in China and Vietnam don't confuse economic with political liberty, but stand by their races against others. Democracies like Japan and South Korea grant freedoms and fraternity for their races foremost. Nationalism matters more than political systems.

Japan allows foreigners to work or study in Japan and foreigners there long enough can obtain permanent residency, but the criteria to obtain citizenship are high. Few of the two million or so foreign residents bother applying. Most numerous among the immigrant citizens are Japanese-born Koreans, whose forebears arrived when Japan ruled Korea before 1945, often involuntarily to work.

A 1984 amendment to the Japanese Nationality Act clarified that race, not place of birth, underpins citizenship. Japan responded to its low birth rate by opening its doors to immigrants, but only those racially Japanese, wholly or substantially. They descended from Japanese émigrés who set out to settle in Japan's and Europe's grand empires. They might have lived overseas, most notably in Latin America, for generations, but are still allowed home.

We see them as South Americans dancing the salsa in street parades, but they could become courteous geisha girls serving green tea in Tokyo gardens by reason of their race. In a very small way, for they make up a very small percentage of the Japanese population, their return gives Japan a little multiculturalism without multiracialism.

When we laud our new-found multiculturalism and say nothing of race, we reduce people to their most visible behaviour: language, cuisine, style of dance. Other races don't. Only once have I read of a Japanese businessman contemplating increasing immigration to Japan to redress its ageing population, but that was on carefully controlled terms. Japan remains Japanese. Japan exists.

Speaking at the Kyushu National Museum in Dazaifu in 2005, future prime minister Tarō Asō said Japan was "one nation, one civilization, one language, one culture, and one race." The Ainu are indigenous to Japan, but Japanese do not defer to them any more than to immigrants, while Colonial Europeans defer to both.

My friend Don (with his Chinese girlfriend) went so far as to call the Japanese the most racist people on earth, in a message to me after I'd lamented another *Crikey* daily mail article blaming racist white Australians for something. In his deferential way, Don intended a gentle rebuke. Japanese might be more obvious than other races with their racism because of their material wealth, peace, and security. We have much less peace and security, but we do have material wealth.

Accepting refugees from other races isn't a universal norm. Like the rest of our interracial immigration, it's a uniquely new Western norm.

As only the West could, Amnesty International issued a report in 2010 complaining that Malaysia was unwelcoming and dangerous for refugees. Malaysian police and the People's Volunteer Corps detained, extorted, and beat refugees "*in effect treated like criminals.*"

In much of the world, people entering or remaining in a country illegally *are* criminals. They don't cease being criminals by claiming refugee status.

Amnesty wanted Malaysia to ratify the 1951 United Nations Convention Relating to the Status of Refugees and grant refugees and asylum seekers the legal status, identity documents, rights to work, access to lawyers, and means of appeal the West gives them. There wasn't a chance of that happening. Amnesty made one recommendation that might be accepted: it wanted the West to accept more refugees from Malaysia. That other countries don't accept immigrants becomes more reason for the West to grant refuge.

Very few countries outside the West have signed the refugee convention. Those that have, like South Korea accepting North Korean refugees, interpret it narrowly. Others harbour those they can't keep out, but give them none of the rights we do. They await Western hospitality.

There was a time we advocated Western countries accepting refugees on the basis we too might need asylum one day, but there's no reason to imagine we'd receive asylum from any country that wouldn't accept us to work or spend money. There's no reciprocity.

My Hong Kong Chinese friend Ted complained sorely when the Australian government announced in 2007 that Australia would take fewer Sudanese because of their high rates of crime. (In fact, the government played politics. No reduction in the Sudanese intake eventuated.) Fond as I am of Ted, I've never heard him advocate China taking refugees.

The only refugees China has allowed to settle have been fellow Chinese fleeing Vietnam from 1979 to '82 due to conflict between the two countries (along with a tiny number of Vietnamese, no more than two percent of the total number of refugees, travelling with them). More than three decades onward, China still denies them citizenship.

If a catastrophe enveloped us or multiculturalism or anything else drove us from our homes, Ted would have somewhere to go. He's intelligent and educated, with a Chinese wife and daughter, but my family couldn't go with them to China. If refugees were white people, the West would care less about them, but if a Western country were to accept me, it would also accept Ted. If a Western country won't take my family and me, carrying our books and pictures with us if we can, we'll have nowhere to go.

In December 2019, Mongolia first offered citizenship to a refugee, after judo champion Saeid Mollaei said he felt afraid to return to Iran. Born in Iran to Azerbaijanis, Mollaei had exposed the pressure on him from Iranian officials to lose his semi-final at the 2019 World Championships in Tokyo so as to avoid a final match against an Israeli. The Mongolian president was also chairman of the Mongolian Judo Federation.

The only Asian countries accepting refugees from resettlement camps are Japan and Korea, but the numbers are miniscule. In 2014, they numbered just twenty-three and fourteen respectively, according to the United Nations High Commissioner of Refugees. Those countries don't give them citizenship or much else.

The first day in October 2015, Prime Minister Najib Razak told the United Nations General Assembly that Malaysia would accept three thousand fellow Muslims as migrants over three years from the millions of refugees from the Syrian Civil War. It expressed Malaysia's desire to lead a Muslim world divided between Shia and Sunni.

Japan explicitly rejects economic refugees, drawn to it by its wealth. We might say the same words, but find so many other reasons for granting rights of refuge they needn't admit money is their motivation. When New York and London banks became less attractive places to work than those in Sydney during the financial crisis of 2008, we described the bankers bound for Australia as refugees. It made them like Asian and African asylum seekers.

If we want to imagine what our countries would've been like without interracial immigration, we could consider Japan. We too could've shared our prosperity with our people, maintaining our cities and towns. (Ours would have had more open spaces than has Japan.) We'd have weathered natural disasters without widespread looting, as did Japan with the Tōhoku earthquake and tsunami in 2011.

Where there's no immigration, there's no xenophobia. With racial homogeneity, there's no problem with racism. It's easy to forget Japan lost World War II.

6. DEMOCRACY

"I am not an Athenian or a Greek, but a citizen of the world," said philosopher Socrates thousands of years ago, according to the historian Plutarch and a wall in the Museum of Australian Democracy in 2010. What through ages of empires was our sense of seeing and acting worldwide, we've come to interpret as being worldwide. We think that makes us the planet. It makes us no place at all.

The democracy sometimes preached in classical Greece and sometimes practiced in classical Rome wasn't universal. It was democracy for Greeks and Romans, and only particular Greeks and Romans. Democracy was predicated upon individuals with different ideas to express and arguments to expound, which we assumed would reveal a common good. Classical democracy remained for the few for thousands of years, until nationalist democracy took hold.

The West came to enjoy universal suffrage: universal within races and nations. Our governments represented us.

"The world is my country," wrote British-born Thomas Paine, an American revolutionary who published *The Rights of Man* in 1791, *"all mankind are my brethren, and to do good is my religion."* The American Revolution was nevertheless nationalistic. American democracy remained racist until the Fifteenth Amendment to the Constitution in 1870, if not the Voting Rights Act of 1965.

The French Revolution too was fundamentally nationalistic. The crime for which the new regime executed King Louis XVI in 1793 was high treason.

Until 1945, we only contemplated democracy within nations. Our postmodern West only contemplates democracy without them.

Like everything else political, democracy is racial. "In multiracial societies," former Singaporean prime minister Lee Kuan Yew told *Der Spiegel* magazine in 2005, "you don't vote in accordance with your economic interests and social interests. You vote in accordance with race and religion."

In 2010, Rahm Emanuel sought election as mayor of Chicago. "I like to vote for Jewish people," said Norm Levin, president of the Great Vest Side Club, "but if they're sort of negative on Israel, they lose me." Levin guaranteed his loyalty to Jews loyal to other Jews.

Some Jews aren't loyal. "I'm sort of hostile to Israel," said resident James Alter.

White people can't vote for our own without defending ourselves from charges of racism. Other races can. If it's not racial loyalty, it's a sense that candidates from their race understand and represent them better than candidates from another. Candidates from other races must offer more to assist them and their race to win their support.

We respect other races voting for their own because they're their own, among whatever considerations they take into account. We cater to it.

The Liberal Party put up Helen Sham Ho for the New South Wales Legislative Council for the Chinese money she brought in. It couldn't have been for her public speaking I once heard.

At three New South Wales by-elections the third Saturday of October 2008, the party fielded candidates selected, at least in part, for their race and religion. In the racially pluralistic Ryde electorate, the party only got as far as an Italian, Victor Dominello. In predominantly Vietnamese Cabramatta, it selected Dai Le. In predominantly Middle Eastern Lakemba, it selected Michael Hawatt, who the Australian Broadcasting Corporation election website described as being *"from the locally important Lebanese Muslim community."* That was to say, he was Lebanese Muslim.

The party polled better than it had polled in previous elections. A little more than a week later, my local state parliamentarian credited that in part to it fielding "candidates that represented the local community." Since two of the three candidates hadn't lived in their respective electorates for years, he wasn't talking about their places of residence. Representative democracy is representation by race.

Many voters choose political parties more than local candidates anyway, which explains anyone but Filipinos voting for Jaymes Diaz in the 2013 Australian election. His breathtaking ignorance of Liberal Party policy made him an international laughing stock, after which he dared not brave a candidates' forum in Greenway.

Outside my local polling booth the day of that election, Benny told me he'd joined the Labour Party while at an Australian university during the era of South African apartheid because "I'm not Anglo-Saxon." (He might've thought I, being white, hadn't noticed.) He associated the Labour Party with everyone who's not Anglo-Saxon, in spite of those Liberal Party candidates who weren't. He was Chinese.

In democracy without nationalism, the most important issues are demographic. In multiracial democracies, the first issue is race.

Ethnic community leaders band together on their concerted behalf. Racial blocs vote according to their racial interests, as they perceive them to be. For all the criticism we mete out upon ourselves, an adage in Australian politics is that racial minorities vote for their race but, all else being equal, prefer Anglo-Saxon candidates to those from other races. They're not as obliging to each other as we are to all of them. We treat them better than they treat each other.

On the rare moments I've been privy to such debate, people like my insurance lawyer friend Jane early in the 1990s cited immigration as an example of why public policy shouldn't defer to public opinion. She wanted a single world government, a very Western thing to want: the logical consequence of open borders.

What we used to call Western democracy, we now condemn for being populism: expressing the will of the people. (Populism is democracy for white people.) Only Western governments don't see their primary responsibility being to safeguard their citizenry. That would be nationalism. We live knowing we have no one on our side, no one in our corner. That's individualism.

Our ideals became universal. Recasting the meaning of our liberal democracies to be non-discriminatory, without favour to our own, Western governments redefined their roles from representing their citizenry to representing the world. We enact treaties and laws placing the world's interests above those of our countries, governing our bits of geography on the world's behalf. We lecture foreign governments what we think they should do but, for the most part, we lead by example. Our visions of a new earth begin with us.

Other countries refuse foreign intervention in their internal affairs. We no longer have the concept of internal affairs, not for anything important.

Foreign affairs are their governments expressing the wills of their people to the rest of the world. Our governments impose the views of the world on our people. Nationalism subordinates foreign relations to national interests. The West subordinates national interests to foreign relations.

We redefined our democracies to be no longer the wills of our nations, but the will of the world. Ours are global democracies, representing all peoples' interests: democracy without discrimination. Ours are still "government of the people, by the people, for the people," in the words of President Abraham Lincoln at Gettysburg in 1863, but we aren't the people anymore. We've handed rule to everyone else.

Australian Greens Party leader Bob Brown neatly expressed our vision delivering the third annual Green Oration in the Hobart Town Hall the fourth Friday in March, 2012. "Fellow Earthians," he began, "for comprehensive earth action, an all-of-the-earth representative democracy is required." It would be "a global parliament" based upon "one planet, one person, one vote, one value."

Many a Western business leader shares the dream of a worldwide superstate for the limitless markets of labour and buyers, which critics of capitalism would let businesspeople have in return for their social laws. The only thing better for business than a single world government would be a single world government failing.

Accustomed as the West is to ruling the world, we presume world government would be our plaything to shape. It wouldn't be. There aren't enough of us. Most of the world doesn't particularly want democracy, as we understand it.

A parliament made up of the world's opinions imposed on all people would promptly eradicate the rights we hold dear. Brown, a homosexual, would find a global parliament discriminating against him. Conversely, tobacco companies would be free again be peddle their poisons to Western children. It might tax away the homes of those rich white people who enabled it or requisition those homes to be hostels.

Global self-determination is no self-determination. There might never be a second earth-wide election.

Brown's vision was exclusionary anyway, given his speech

included his belief in life on other planets. He thought our "many predecessors in the cosmos…brought about their…downfall" by failing to deal with environmental issues. (They might just have come up with planet-wide elections.)

In the absence of global elections, Western governments interpret the world's will and interests. Most, if not all, races have political classes whose opinions prevail above their compatriots. Only the Western elite subjugate their races to others. We pay regard to what the United Nations and assemblies of bureaucrats would have us do; the West becomes their laboratory. Judging by the enthusiasm with which other races take up the chances we give them, they're probably right.

There is no international community. There's simply a Western elite with a remarkably uniform world view. We're the only races subscribing.

That we embarked upon our single-world vision without the approval of our race only makes us prouder. In his memoirs, former prime minister Malcolm Fraser said he knew he risked a backlash from the Australian electorate by admitting Vietnamese refugees in the late 1970s, fundamentally changing the country.

Having been a teenager through those years, I knew he got away with it by never fighting elections on immigration. He won two elections with the good fortune of not being the previous prime minister. He won a third by frightening the electorate that a new government would introduce a capital gains tax. (Australians hated taxation even more than we hated immigration.)

Interpreting much from democratic elections is difficult; people have all sorts of reasons to vote as they do. They might disagree or agree with candidates on issues, but still vote or not vote for them. We normally don't know their second and subsequent preferences. All we can say is that in no referendum or election has a majority of white people clearly and consciously voted for increased interracial immigration. Governments overrode us.

Democracy is a right we enjoy. We don't have the democracy, we have the right: the right to make choices we're supposed to make, from most options the same. We think we're democratic for being able to vote for whomever we want to vote, from what seems an array of choices, but our elections are confined to the choices before us: between candidates who need only position themselves to one side of another, subject to the best marketing they can buy.

Western governments operate beyond democracy's reach. The practical reality of Western democracy has long left our ancient ideals to become competitive deception. Without nationalism, Western leaders ceased representing their nations. They represent themselves. Our politicians don't look beyond the next periodic election dates by which they're judged. They'll have retired before babies born today vote. We can only blame the people for some of our governments and fewer still of our laws.

We dwell upon our individual beliefs and pursuits. Unsuited to individualism, democracy hasn't ensured good government, at least since the Second World War. Democracy depends upon nationalism.

The British Empire brought democracy to the Fijian islands, but democratic process didn't make dispossession easier for Fijians to bear. Nor did more than a century sharing their island group help them become used to the idea. During the nineteenth century, we brought thousands of Indian labourers because Fijians didn't labour enough for us. Descendants of those immigrants dressed and ate much as Fijians did, but weren't Fijian.

Particularly during the late twentieth century, many Fijians emigrated to Australian and New Zealand. By 1987, the proportion of Fijians had fallen to about half Fiji's population. The perception that Fijian Indians dominated the democratically elected government, disenfranchising Fijians, led to a military coup.

We might be Europeans whose families have been in Australasia or the Americas for centuries, or in Europe forever, but the wonder remains that we don't feel at least a little of the same. We're the only race willing to be ruled by others, accepting of demographic destinies.

Western governments aren't so racist as to intervene to protect white people unless, perhaps, they happen to be their citizenry, but the Indian government loyally spoke up to defend the rights and interests of Fijian Indians, whatever their citizenship. Born faraway, they did so by race.

So, for that matter, did we. Without regard for race, Australia and New Zealand governments wanted democracy in Fiji, whoever it brought to power and the prime ministership.

Indians and other immigrants with citizenship of Western countries can count on two governments to promote their interests. White people can't count on any. Oh, we might speak up on behalf of our citizenry in trouble somewhere, but little more than we say on behalf of other citizenry in trouble. By deeming us citizens of everywhere, we become citizens of nowhere.

A second military coup in 1987 removed the British monarchy from Fiji and established a republic, which didn't bother us. (We might even have liked it.) Several more coups and mutinies occurred thereafter, with Fijians taking solace from the exodus of Indians exceeding the exodus of Fijians.

Fijians and other races alter their systems of government to protect their political power. We alter our systems to reduce ours.

If the law is a creature with a mind, then the creature is parliamentary and judicial decree. Our doctrine of the separation of powers presumes that parliaments pass laws and courts interpret them, subject in some countries to a constitution. The common law is a British tradition of judges making law to fill lacuna that parliament hasn't filled. When parliament fills it, the common law falls away.

One view holds that judges settle upon what their decisions should be. They then set about justifying them.

Increasingly since the Second World War, Western governments and courts have imposed their vision of what liberal democracies should be, as if that's what our nation makers intended, but it's very different (if not diametrically opposed) to anything our nation makers envisaged. When judges (not normally answerable to democratic elections) ceased expressing national visions but sectional or global visions, their independence ceased being a cornerstone of national democracy. It became an impediment to it.

Half the thirty thousand residents of Port Chester, New York, being Hispanic hadn't elected any Hispanics to the six trustee seats by 2006, which Judge Stephen Robinson held breached the Voting Rights Act. He rejected an American government plan to create six voting districts with one focused upon the Hispanic neighbourhoods, but approved a system known as cumulative voting, in our euphemistic dance around mentioning race. White Americans continued casting one vote each at the election in June 2010. Hispanics could each cast six.

The election research and reform group hired to consult in Port Chester called itself Fair Vote, as if fairness means discrimination against white people. Amy Ngai, a director at Fair Vote, believed Hispanics having six votes each remedied the discrimination by white voters choosing white candidates, although I'm unaware of any evidence that white voters predicated their choices on race as Hispanics could. She was unconcerned about the discrimination of Hispanic voters choosing Hispanic candidates.

Randolph McLaughlin represented a plaintiff in the lawsuit before Robinson. He said the idea was "to create a system whereby the Hispanic community would be able to nominate and elect a candidate of their choice."

If it seemed white Americans were abandoning popular democracy (as we once understand democracy to be), they weren't. They already had. Cumulative voting was already in place to elect school boards in Amarillo, Texas, county commissions in Chilton County, Alabama, and the city council in Peoria, Illinois, but not to boost white people's representation. We're reverting to democracy with discrimination, but our new discrimination favours others.

We don't just accept racial democracy empowering other races. We accelerate it.

Hispanic candidates in Port Chester could be as biased as the discriminatory democracy in which they stood. "I hope that if Hispanics get in, they do something for all the Hispanic people," said Candida Sandoval, in Spanish.

It worked. Luis Marino, a school district maintenance director, was elected a trustee.

We're not the only race on earth denoting rights by race. We are the only race doing so at our expense.

7. BOUNDARIES

During one of my trips to London through the 1990s, an Englishman told me how he thought Prime Minister John Major could overcome poor opinion polling and win the next general election. (In our democratic individualism, elections had become battles between party leaders.) Major would offer the voters a referendum on the United Kingdom withdrawing from the European Union. For the chance to have their country back, an enthusiastic populace would re-elect him.

Like other races of the world we respect so much, we hold natures within us. Some part of us (poorly neglected of late) yearns to be a people in a country around us. Our yearning might be unrequited, but it's yearning nevertheless. Denying people their innate desires to live among their kind would be oppression, unless we're the people.

Major never made the offer. He lost the 1997 election to Tony Blair, who'd offered the Scots and Welsh a little semblance of their countries with referenda on parliamentary devolution. Far from satisfying the Scots, devolution furthered the movement for Scottish independence. The English continued complaining louder than other Europeans complained about being part of the European Union, but almost two decades would pass before a Conservative Party prime minister trying to retain power promised such a referendum.

Michael managed Holyman Limited's interests in Europe. Tall, confident, and most assured, he was born into privilege and pleased to remain there. He spoke well and practiced good manners, as I'm sure he'd have done before attending a Swiss finishing school in his youth.

Holyman's London offices were in Covent Garden, where in a conversation one day Michael corrected me for using the term "Continental Europeans." Sometime since I was young, Britons like Michael decided Britain and Ireland were parts of the European continent.

photographs for five dollars each.

Having checked the photographs at both tables, I returned to the first. "They're five dollars, too?" I checked.

"They're not with us," said one of the men tersely. "We're the official photographers – they just went in. We need to talk to someone about it."

People were much too polite to say anything more, but being official photographers hadn't meant anything. Our doctrinaire devotion to free market competition meant the official and intruder photographers all packed up unsold photographs at the end of the night. It was photographic anarchy, highly inefficient, but also unfair to the official photographers who lost income to the intruders.

Nobody else seemed to care, but I paid ten dollars for my photograph from the official photographers. (I'd not seen any pictures of me among those still for sale among the unofficial ones, anyway.)

We can hardly blame immigrants for thinking our houses are similarly open. My youngest daughter told Chinese girls Grace and Maya they couldn't play in our front garden, the first day of December 2013, but still they played. They opened our west-side neighbours' gate, and played in their front garden with their dog Rango. About the only home Grace didn't feel she could enter was her own; her parents told her to play elsewhere, because she was noisy. Her parents hadn't opened their country to all comers either.

Jews understand the need for geopolitical boundaries as regards Israel. Arabs demand unemployed foreigners leave their countries. Asians understand boundaries, even if they disagree where they lie. Black African boundaries are often tribal, with national boundaries often artificial, but they're boundaries nevertheless. The boundaries nobody respects are Western.

Hidden away from our postmodern dogma is McCaskey East High School in Lancaster, Pennsylvania. Unusually, maybe even uniquely in 2011 America, the school separated black students from other students in their homerooms, albeit for only six minutes a day and twenty minutes twice a month. (It also separated black boys from black girls, but that was less controversial; gender is less controversial than race, in the West.) Some students, staff, and parents opposed those brief moments of segregation, saying it ran against everything the school stood for. (Integration, whatever the consequence, is about all the West stands for.)

Principal Bill Jimenez admitted that no other students were divided by race at the school. He defended the approach because academic data showed black students performing worse than other students. "One of the things we said when we did this was: 'Let's look at the data, let's not run from it. Let's confront it and see what we can do about it.'" In a West that insists everyone's equal, whatever the data, he was remarkably brave.

Angela Tilghman, an instructional coach at the school, said statistics showed only about a third of McCaskey's black students scored proficient or advanced in reading in the 2010 Pennsylvania System of School Assessment tests, compared with forty-two percent of students overall and sixty percent of white students. In mathematics, only twenty-seven percent of black students scored proficient or advanced. She said research had shown that grouping black students by gender with a strong role model could boost academic achievement and self-esteem.

It begged the question whether other races might also need racial role models: mentors from their race. White students might too.

At least to some degree and in some ways, races fare better with boundaries. In the 1930s, the United States Communist Party wanted to carve out a black state encompassing Mississippi and Alabama. Black Americans had little interest in that one.

Joseph Stalin might've killed only Georgians or never come to power at all without the Union of Soviet Socialist Republics. It allowed him to kill tens of millions of people far and wide.

National governments are safer not because governments are safer, but because nations are safer. National borders are in people's best interests.

Globalist ideology demanded Soviet citizens be loyal to their communist superstate instead of the nominally autonomous republics comprising it, but the last leader of the Soviet Union, Mikhail Gorbachev, recognised that those republics were based upon race. As well as republics for the Armenians, Azerbaijanis, and so forth, regions within those republics were dedicated to racial minorities like Tartars, Jews, and Chukchi Indians. Sympathetic to African Americans, Puerto Ricans, and Poles, Gorbachev proposed America set aside states for them in 1987.

Black lawmakers found Gorbachev's proposal "somewhat

offensive," but anyone believing white racism denies other races jobs, housing, and other services should welcome racially dedicated states. White Americans could send money over the borders.

For all their cries, if we really believed the problems of indigenous races were our fault because we've come (but not the fault of recent immigrants because we'd already come), then we'd denote their tribal homelands national borders. We don't. We do whatever's the simplest for us to assist them.

I'm not aware of any collectivist culture that isn't racially homogenous. I'm only aware of the multiracial communism that failed. Even Cuba, that model of post-racial communism, failed (as dictator Fidel Castro admitted late in life), in spite of the 1958 revolutionaries inheriting so prosperous a country.

Not only communists wanted separation between races. Among the many surprising tracts of information I've stumbled across from computer sites, few rivalled my disbelief when I first read of Abraham Lincoln's overt racism.

Lincoln condemned slavery, but not racism. "There is a natural disgust in the minds of nearly all white people to the idea of indiscriminate amalgamation of the white and black races," he told an audience at Springfield, Illinois, on the twenty-sixth day of June 1857, four years before America's Civil War began. Ironically (given he waged the Civil War to hold the Union together), Lincoln was arguing against the Union admitting a slave state, Kansas.

Historian Phillip Magness, an author of *Colonisation after Emancipation: Lincoln and the Movement for Black Resettlement* in 2011, found documents in British archives showing Lincoln did more than toy with the idea of sending freed slaves from America. For at least a year after signing his proclamation outlawing slavery in the Confederacy, he took measures preparing settlements in the British colonies that later became Belize and Guyana. Black colonisation had already been attempted and aborted in what became Panama and on an island off Haiti, where several hundred freed slaves arrived in 1862 before the settlement failed a year later. Early that century, the American Colonisation Society had organised efforts to ship thousands of black Americans to the Liberian colony in Africa.

Magness believed Lincoln couldn't conceive a biracial democracy and wanted to avoid racial conflict in America. With four million blacks in America at the time, it's interesting to imagine at what cost and effort Lincoln was willing to keep free peoples apart.

Historian Michael Burlingame, chair of Lincoln Studies at the University of Illinois at Springfield in 2011, believed Lincoln's public actions were "the way to sugar-coat the emancipation pill." It was the first I'd read of Northerners needing sugar-coating, but they were more concerned about preserving the Union than abolishing slavery. "So many people in the North said we will not accept emancipation, unless it is accompanied by colonisation." That was to say, deportation.

Lincoln seems never to have wavered from his views of black people in white America, even if he had little time to act upon them. "I believe that it would be better to export them all to some fertile country with a good climate," he told General Benjamin Butler on the fifteenth day of April 1865, shortly before his death, "which they could have to themselves."

Australia understood. Among the peoples conscripted into poorly paid labour during the nineteenth century, for which food, lodging, and pennies now seem inadequate compensation, were Melanesian Kanaks taken from New Caledonia to Pacific Rim countries and colonies, including the sugar cane plantations of Queensland. Little information about them is available, and I've never heard anyone mention them. When their labour ceased, we returned them to New Caledonia.

Other conscripted labourers didn't return. Formed in 1972, the Australian South Sea Islander United Council obtained for them the rights and benefits of Australia's indigenous peoples. It lobbies for housing, health, and education better than their peoples returned home can get. For the rest, repatriation saved subsequent generations (theirs and ours) from feeling injustice and pains for the past.

Some of the boundaries we now see between countries, our forebears set between empires. Indonesia's borders upon independence in 1949 were the product of European colonialism. Soon, its borders were the product of its own colonialism.

When the Netherlands prepared her colony Western New Guinea for independence, nearby Indonesia threatened to invade. The Dutch prepared to resist, before bowing to American pressure to attend diplomatic talks. The Dutch passed control to a temporary United Nations administration in 1962. Within a year,

Indonesia took over.

We weren't particularly fussed, consumed as we are by opposition to empires only from Europe. We condemn our past imperialism, while condoning other people's present imperialism. Indonesia itself is a Javanese empire at the best of times.

A decade later, the Australian government pressed Portugal to withdraw from her colonial possession East Timor. Following a 1974 revolution, Portugal set about withdrawing from her remaining possessions anyway, but with her looming withdrawal from East Timor in 1975 came civil war. To our great surprise, Indonesian troops invaded East Timor within days after its independence, equipped with Western arms and intelligence and murdering six Australian journalists.

West New Guineans and East Timorese weren't immigrant populations. They were conquered peoples, whose lands Indonesia annexed and Javanese colonised. One colonial ruler replaced another.

Through the ensuing decades, Indonesia poured money, resources, and people into East Timor, but the benefits brought by the colonists couldn't compensate the Timorese for their pains and anger feeling disempowered from their land. No number of fine buildings, improved healthcare, civic order, roads, and other infrastructure ameliorated for the Timorese losing their racial homes, much as we colonial Europeans acknowledge it doesn't for our colonially dispossessed. They'd rather land be their impoverished own than other people's paradise.

As Europeans learned with many of our colonial possessions, East Timor became a greater problem than it was worth. Timorese patriots engaged in guerrilla activity we could have called terrorism, if we weren't so sympathetic. Weary of the festering sore never healing, and with a new Australian government less willing than its predecessors to endorse Indonesian imperialism, Indonesia finally withdrew. East Timor became independent in 2002.

African tribes defend their tribal lands. Arab tribes stake out their sands and emirates. Islanders keep their islands off other people's coasts and in the long-lost South Pacific. Only the West gives ours away.

8. OUR AGE OF ISOLATION

Through the 1990s, I spent much time in America. Americans liked Australians because they thought we were like they used to be, unaware of how hurriedly we were trying to catch up.

In spite of suffering two world wars, by the 1950s and '60s, we had good lives. American neighbourhoods were alive with children, mothers' tennis matches, neighbourhood barbecues, community television nights, and overflowing churches.

Australians left our rear doors open for neighbours to visit, talking with tea at kitchen tables. Among them was the wife of Ben Chifley, a train driver who ultimately became prime minister. She remained at their home in Bathurst, through which Sam Malloy guided my eldest three children and me half a century later. We didn't study as hard as Jews and Asians now study, but we were at least as clever without it.

Older people know what we used to be like, but few facts are more certain to cause outrage than those pointing out we were happier before other races arrived. We came to think good lives were a right, but the more we embraced other races, the less we embraced each other. Our togetherness we offered everyone else, respecting their senses of togetherness we no longer felt for us. We embraced immigration without discrimination, but we can't admit all comers and be a community.

Nationalism is community. When we lost our nations, we lost everything we valued: our land to belong.

There's no global village. Western countries aren't villages of the world. They aren't villages at all. What remains isn't some unified humanity, but individualism. We global citizens turn more to the world but less to our neighbours, holed up in their homes. Ours is the age of isolation.

In his 2010 book *Disconnected*, Australian National University economist Andrew Leigh presented data showing Australians to be living lonelier, less connected lives than thirty to forty years earlier. We're less likely to belong to organisations, participate in civic activities such as casting a valid vote, or volunteer. We're less likely to be part of a church community or play sport. We have fewer friends and fewer connections with neighbours.

In his 1995 essay and 2000 book *Bowling Alone*, Harvard University political scientist Robert Putnam said much the same of America. Trust and reciprocity had declined.

Our lands without borders leave us fearful. A report published in 2009 by the Young Foundation, supported by thirteen major charitable foundations, found the rise of individualism had left millions of Britons unhappy, lonely, and unable to cope with the changes around them. What once was a nation, standing together in war, had become psychologically fragile.

People with strong and supportive communities are happy, although the Young Foundation report never investigated whether people need only think they have such communities. We need each other more than we understand. Increased wealth doesn't mean very much, except for the production of reports.

The gentlest and most civilised tribalism was our quintessentially Western sense of community. Those who weren't there don't know what community was only a generation or two ago. We knew our communities by people the first time we saw them. The eyes of passers-by met and we'd smile. We conversed.

However much we enjoy our friends from whatever race, the real measures of community aren't our relationships with people we know but those with people we don't. It's a collective sense, according us a chance to help and be helped by strangers in a street. Communist Poland in 1986 and free Finland in 1996 and '97 knew community, without threatening me the visitor. I felt more secure there than I've dared feel since then in much of the West.

As Australian journalist Adele Horin in 2010 described the past we love to malign, "*providing you weren't gay or black there was a strong sense of belonging.*" (Homosexuality was rare and blacks had their own belonging.) We now have what she called "*cultural ghettoes,*" namely "*a small circle of the like-minded. Even the once-usual practice of talking to strangers on planes and buses, and of chatting to taxi drivers is dying out. Who can bother with small talk with strangers?*" Unwilling to contemplate race, Horin put much of it down to dual-income families and long working hours. Communities depended on neighbourhood mothers.

Robert Putnam's research revealed racial diversity leads to a

The term "Australasia" had similarly fallen from use, for implying something conjoining Australia to New Zealand without Asia or the Pacific. I've only used it again because of my writing.

On the second Thursday in May 2009, I waited with my second daughter for another appointment with the ear, nose, and throat surgeon who'd inserted grommets into her ears. Browsing about the Adventist Book Centre at the Sydney Adventist Hospital, she looked at the brightly coloured pencils and other stationery. I mulled around the bookshelves. Most books seemed to have only one or two copies available, standing so only their spines were visible, but several copies of one book's bright blue cover faced browsers like me. Clearly fresh and new, they must've recently arrived. Their title was *Boundaries*.

I'd used the word that day, writing about society, and wondered what boundaries the book described. On the back cover, the authors distinguished physical, mental, emotional, and spiritual boundaries, saying we need them for our well-being, happiness, peace of mind, and fulfilment. We need sometimes to say "No."

I couldn't help but think the West is trying to make functioning societies without boundaries. We can't.

I didn't buy the book. My daughter bought, with ten cents of her money, a small golden smiley eraser.

We understand personal property so well when it comes to cars we drive, beds in which we sleep, and even erasers. Private ownership motivates people. Private landholdings secure us; even communist Hungary maintained private ownership of people's homes. We understand ownership of our homes better than our homelands.

Open doors to our countries are open doors to our premises. Neither countries nor private functions are ours.

The fourth Friday of October 2009 saw a dinner in tribute of retiring federal parliamentarian Brendan Nelson, in the ballroom of the Four Seasons Hotel in George Street. It was a huge affair, with former prime minister John Howard and former treasurer Peter Costello among the hundreds of diners, along with photographers taking pictures. Afterwards, two men sat at a long row of white-clothed tables outside the ballroom selling their photographs for ten dollars each.

Across the way from them was another table of photographs, at which two East Asians sat. A hand-scribbled sign offered withdrawal from "collective life." It reduces trust both between races and within them.

Not only did individualism lead the West to pursue racial integration. Other races around us make us more individualistic.

Whether or not multiracialism and multiculturalism are theoretically compatible with being a civilisation, society, or community, they've proven in practice to be incompatible. "*Rising diversity in human societies tends to drive people apart*," wrote political ethnologist Frank Salter in 2010, "*causing them to take sanctuary in individual pursuits and ethnic communities. The practical consequences are reduced public altruism or social capital…and a general loss of trust.*" Community requires racial homogeneity.

Ours are the communities more abstract than real, embracing people of all races alike. We don't imagine them otherwise. I'm not sure what community means the way we've come to speak of it. I'm not sure what we want it to mean. In our geography, it's our presumption that we all get along. It's enough not to be in open warfare.

When my children first attended our local preschool, it carried out Sunday morning working bees. Parents, normally fathers, expended a few hours tending to the gardens, including setting an old, strangely ornamental porcelain toilet bowl in a garden. Parents who didn't attend were supposed to donate fifty dollars in lieu. The only parents helping were white, but the parents not helping weren't donating money. The preschool dispensed with the working bees, levied all parents an additional fifty dollars each term (I think it was), and employed a gardener.

Community groups have come to have less trouble raising funds than they have finding volunteers to carry out chores. A study of 2006 census data for Melbourne by Ernest Healy, senior research fellow at the Centre for Population and Urban Research at Monash University, showed that white Australians and English-speaking immigrants were more likely to volunteer than people from other races, even those born in Australia. We're also far more likely to carry out volunteer work in suburbs with others like us. We tire of assisting people who never reciprocate.

"When you create societies from mixed backgrounds it may not lead to overt violence…but to something scarier, a withdrawal from the civic sphere," said Healy, "a feeling of less connectedness." Immigrant races confine their altruism to their friends, families, and neighbours rather than a "broader social good."

If we think countries can be multicultural, multiracial, then it's because we've become lax in our interpretation of what countries can be. By any substantive meaning of country, connecting people together, there are no multiracial countries.

What were our countries have become lonely places. We grab the friends we can to hold for as long as we can. If one or more among them are from another race, then we think we're better for the racial diversity around us, but we never wonder what friends we might have had in a homogeneous home.

A city doesn't cease being lonely for the friends we make. The spaces between strangers make it lonely. People around us with whom we have no commonality, except perhaps solitude, only make us more alone. People we don't know leave us feeling apart.

For people living alone, every room affirms our solitude. A two-bedroom apartment means a room for a desk, computer, and exercise bicycle. A three-bedroom apartment is a one-bedroom apartment with a study and gymnasium. Saving money to spend on nights out and holidays, we might share accommodation. The best housemates are those that don't intrude on our lives, like nurses on night shifts and airline stewards away for days at a time.

Not content with aloneness, our humanity leaves us lonely. Individuals can't be anything else. Solitude makes us comfortable only when we're separated from humanity. Some people don't become comfortably alone. Perhaps no one does.

Ours is the smallness of one. If we don't live in suburban solitude, we live in rural seclusion.

We don't bother caring for neighbours or what neighbours think of us, when we know we won't be neighbours for long. We deal with each other during economic transactions, and needn't see each other again. Investors needn't meet employees, customers, or suppliers. Company managers needn't revisit the people they've fired. We vote without regard for how our vote affects people we'll never meet. We have our ideals about the way the world and country should be, and never see the citizens that suffer because of them.

If we hark to a village mentality, it's because crowds isolate people that villages don't. Towns rather than cities, houses rather than tower blocks, are the best places for people to live. People knowing each other aside from their trade (or knowing people who know each other) see their political decisions and economic transactions in terms of whom they affect. Self-interest requires thought of morality among people who might encounter each other again. The only ideals worth holding are those we're willing to bring down on ourselves, as freely as we're willing to bring them down upon others.

No longer are we the community in which I lived as a child. I grew up in a suburban neighbourhood, where we knew neighbours and strangers were kind, ready to help. They included neighbours from New Zealand, Oklahoma, and Bermuda, racially all British.

There were few Asians at school. Most of them were my friends. Our schools were British.

Community wasn't universal. It was another Western trait we lost.

My children, born since 1996, are growing up without community or country. They don't know neighbourhood. Strangers stay strangers who won't answer the door. There are no invitations to morning organic tea with pickle whole-wheat sandwiches. We know a handful of families through our children's activities, as well as one or two of the children whose parents leave them alone to play by the road.

Our open arms to the world haven't brought us community with the Vietnamese family living nearby or Koreans across the road, while we've lost it with our neighbours like us. We have friends and small relationships, but they're born of individuals.

To those of us immersed in our tiny, little lives, losing community doesn't matter. A Neighbourhood Watch Area in St Ives polled its residents to confirm they didn't want to meet each other. They wanted to receive newsletters reporting on crime, doubtlessly distributed by electronic and other mail preventing other recipients from identifying them. We buy burglar alarm systems, and want our neighbours to leave us alone.

In a generation or two, we've become the most solitary people on earth. Amidst all that we have – our ideals and riches – we're alone. We sit in our thick leather armchairs beneath sprawling wall paintings, condemned by our politics of globalism: individualism.

We have cuisine without kindness, Feng Shui without friends. We live in solitary confinement.

We've become like elderly Elsie Brown, estranged from her

husband and neighbours, living in a few dark rooms at the rear of an old dry-cleaning store in Bentleigh in Melbourne. "When I was a kid, we knew everyone in the street by name," said her neighbour Maurice Hadley in March 2003. "Now you can live in a place for twenty-seven years, and you only know your neighbours on either side."

Brown's unpaid water bills had led police to break into her home. In a blanket on a couch, where she'd died of natural causes, they found her body rotting. From the newspapers and letters around her, police concluded she'd lain there, unnoticed, for twenty-three months.

9. THE COSTS OF DIVERSITY

Western borders are open to anyone willing to work or spend. Either will do.

Throughout the West, we're mindlessly convinced immigration provides economic benefits. In the course of writing this book, I was surprised to discover academic literature about the economic costs of immigration and multiculturalism, such as those by German political sociologist Christian Joppke. They remain obscure and without influence, unable to get onto television or into newspapers, at least that I've seen. (My work might also prove inconsequential.)

Our selective economics means we obsess with economic growth and disregard the costs, including those that economic analyses don't consider. We individuals care only about the costs of immigration to us, not our countries and compatriots, but nation states are in people's individual and collective interests.

Much of the problem comes from our refusal to distinguish between races, and between past and present. Our colonial forebears conquered frontiers, building countries. Present-day immigrants are the easy immigrants, coming to countries already in place, with jobs, charities, and government payments. They occupy homes, hospitals, and schools already built or that we build for them. Our doctrine of the individual credits them with coming to improve their lives. We're no longer building nations, why would they?

Economist Henry Ergas in 2010 supported immigration, but acknowledged the problems. Immigration increases prices to buy or use public assets, which can exclude local people from them altogether. When those assets are overseas owned, not even the high prices benefit local people. He gave the example of a public swimming pool, although I thought of the houses my children won't be able to buy. Building more swimming pools isn't a simple solution, because the unit costs of doing so are often higher than those of existing capacity. It also increases prices.

"*Specifically,*" Ergas went onto say, "*nothing saps integration more than the welfare state, which can make it optional for migrants to find their way in the local society and labour market. Little wonder the great miracles of migrant absorption occurred in the Australia of the 1950s and 1960s, when income transfers barely existed.*" (The migrants absorbed in the 1950s and '60s were Europeans.) "*And little wonder Europe is now trapped in migrant ghettos and rampant xenophobia.*"

Some of the most profound remarks of the twentieth century came from economists, quiet apart from their relevance to economics. "One of the great mistakes is to judge policies and programmes by their intentions rather than their results," said American economist Milton Friedman in 1975. He could've been speaking about any number of idyllic visions for our postmodern West.

At the Institute for Liberty and Policy Analysis' annual World Libertarian Conference in Costa Rica in August 1999, Friedman explained why America shouldn't have opened her borders to all. "I am in favour of the unilateral reduction of tariffs, but the movement of goods is a substitute for the movement of people. As long as you have a welfare state, I do not believe you can have a unilateral open immigration. I would like to see a world in which you could have open immigration, but stop kidding yourselves. On the other hand, the welfare state does not prevent unilateral free trade. I believe that they are in different categories."

Free trade doesn't require immigration. Countries outside the West understand.

We work to pay taxes funding payments to strangers traversing the world to receive them. Friedman would've tolerated immigration that gave immigrants no right to welfare. "If you could do that, that would be fine," he said, "but I don't believe you can do that. It's not only that it is not politically feasible. I don't think that it is desirable to have two classes of citizens in a society. We want a free society."

Friedman's analysis would allow bilateral immigration between countries with similar welfare arrangements. At least on that issue, people have no less incentive to enter local society and work in one country than the other.

Immigration stimulates economic activity, which we want it to do, not just in big cities and suburbs but regional centres and towns: everywhere there's a businessperson looking to grow. Not content with what we already have, we want more customers and suppliers with whom to trade. Only one from the millions of immigrants needs to reach us to make it worthwhile. "More workers meant more consumption," said demographer Bernard Salt in 2010, of Australia's booming population after World War II, "more people competing for property and, importantly, more tax."

Consumption doesn't make us happier and competition is stress, but we'll support anything we think means paying less tax. "While immigration needs to be managed with better infrastructure," said demographer Brian Haratsis in 2010, "we also need high immigration for sound economic reasons. If we don't, we'll all end up paying higher taxes."

The problem is: it isn't true. If it used to be true, it no longer is.

Any fiscal benefits of immigration are, at best, temporary. Young immigrants might pay more money in taxes than they receive in government welfare and services, but they age and have children, ultimately consuming more than they contribute. A 2013 report by University College London economists calculated that recent immigrants paid more in tax than they consumed in public services, but that immigrants who'd arrived in the 1980s and '90s, stayed, and had children were paying only eighty-five pence for every pound of services they consumed.

National governments allow immigration. State and local governments bear the immediate costs. Modern-day immigration leaves local people worse off because we incur the costs in money and labour of additional housing, transport, and so forth. Still, we suffer crowding and congestion. We provide healthcare when immigrants fall sick, and when they don't. Educating children from undeveloped countries (redressing their years without education) costs more than educating those from other Western countries. Without spending that money, standards fall, prices rise.

Governments expending the proceeds of taxation upon immigrants increase the tax burden upon local people, who receive less government benefit. If taxpayers don't immediately bear the costs imposed, then governments compound their levels of debt.

Any benefits of immigration are tiny, and not for local people. The Australian Productivity Commission's research report *Economic Impacts of Immigration and Population Growth*, issued in April 2006, found "*the effect of increased skilled migration on average living standards is projected to be positive, but small.*" The increase in income per person was far less than could be gained from measures to increase workforce productivity. *"It is also likely that most of the benefits accrue to the immigrants themselves."*

"English language proficiency stands out as a key factor determining the ease of settlement and labour market success of immigrants," said the report. Large numbers of immigrants aren't proficient.

Host nations incur the costs of producing materials in a myriad of languages. A letter I received from Ryde City Council inviting people to comment on a proposed supermarket wasn't merely in English, but also in Arabic, Armenian, Chinese, Farsi, Italian, and Korean. Anyone still not understanding the letter could speak to the council, which would engage a translation and interpretation service.

Courtrooms, counsellors, and everyone else dealing with immigrants require those services. We need yet more immigrants to translate their words for us and our words for them.

Western immigrants are much cheaper to accommodate than others. In 2015, Royal Life Saving New South Wales paid for up to nine swimming lessons plus tuition for immigrant adults from the Middle East, Africa, and South East Asia because they were less likely than other adults to know how to swim.

Along with charities, all levels of government expend great time and money trying to engage young people of particular races (in Australia, primarily Arabs and Pacific Islanders) with clubs and other associations, hoping to keep them from crime. It's clearly not working for all of them. Reverend Laurel at our family's Uniting church in August 2014 blamed the failures among Tongans not upon Tongans, but upon the programmes running out of money.

Multiracial workforces are more difficult to manage than homogenous ones, with additional costs of communication and implementing change. Educating workers about workplace safety obligations means more than just information brochures and guidelines in their languages. Regulators in Victoria and Western Australia offer guidance notes and in New South Wales an assistance programme on how to communicate health and safety matters to workers not speaking English.

In 2010, the New South Wales Industrial Relations Commission fined the East Sun Building Pty Ltd eighty thousand dollars after scaffolding collapsed on a residential construction project, seriously injuring a worker. The commission ordered the company to publicise its conviction and warnings of the risks of construction work in newspapers in the languages representing the nationalities predominantly undertaking finishing trades in the Australian construction industry: English, Spanish, Korean, Cantonese, and Mandarin.

We beg for more immigration for the sake of our profits. We palm the costs onto willing governments, which pass them along to unwilling ratepayers and taxpayers who can't see what's behind their rates and taxes. The costs of a multiracial workforce that governments don't bear are borne by businesses and customers.

In 2013, twelve Hispanic custodians complained of discrimination by the Auraria Higher Education Centre of the Metro State University in Denver. It became a full investigation by the Equal Employment Opportunity Commission. "If I could speak English I wouldn't have the problems that exist," said Bertha Ribota. She claimed she was injured at work, because she couldn't read a warning sign in English.

The Hispanics accused the Auraria campus of deliberately leaving employees that only spoke Spanish ignorant of the terms and conditions of their employment, safety, and more. "What is sort of a neutral business practice, that they speak English on campus and it's an English-only campus, has a discriminatory impact on this group of workers," argued attorney Tim Markham.

The Auraria campus believed employees should understand basic English. "It's not our goal to provide every document translated or every conversation translated," said spokesman Blaine Nickeson. "Our employees are expected to interact with members of the public, and that interaction we expect them to be able to understand English."

In 2008, a Britain's House of Lords committee report *The Economic Impact of Immigration* confirmed the economic reality: even record levels of immigration had "little or no impact" on Britain's economic well-being. "Population increases make countries bigger, but they don't make countries more prosperous," said former chancellor Nigel Lawson.

Former Australian Treasury secretary John Stone wrote in 2010 of the claim that immigration provided economic benefit. "*About forty-five years ago the then Secretary to the Treasury, Sir Richard (Dick) Randall, asked me to draft a Treasury paper on the economic effects of immigration. Randall, a strong supporter of our then immigration policies (as was I), believed such a paper would conclude that they produced real economic benefits. Weeks later, having struggled – with my small staff – to produce that paper, I told Randall that we could not honestly reach that conclusion. While immigration produced a larger labour force, and hence a greater rate of growth of total Gross Domestic Product (GDP), we could not show that it raised per capita GDP – the average Australian's living standard. While the immigrants were almost invariably better off, existing Australians were if anything marginally worse off. Despite many attempts since by interested parties to prove the contrary, I have never seen an intellectually rigorous study that did so."*

Neither have I. *"In short,"* continued Stone, *"immigration does not improve average Australians' living standards, and that long-standing argument for it has no substance. Our corporate chieftains – including importantly those controlling our media – find that conclusion unacceptable. More immigrants mean more demand for their products, whether widgets or newspapers. Thus, when the latter editorialise about the need for large (and preferably larger) immigration programs 'in the national interest,' they should declare their own."*

Immigration harms the host nation. Bob Birrell, director of the Centre for Population and Urban Research at Monash University, saw immigration as an economic drain on all Australians. "Melbourne is a parasite economy," he said in 2010. "Increasingly, the fiscal dividend from Australia's mineral boom is having to be distributed to Victoria to pay for the needs of Melbourne's population boom."

"In other words," wrote journalist Paul Sheehan, *"Melbourne is growing for the sake of growing, racing towards a population of 5 million, using other people's money."*

Birrell and his colleague Ernest Healy were the authors of a paper concluding, *"The Labor government's high immigration policy has little to do with the skill needs of the resources industry… By far the greatest beneficiaries of high immigration are the immigrants, not the resident population. High immigration lowers per capita productivity growth, a key to sustainable growth. It retards the growth of per capita wealth. It accelerates the rate of food importation. (Australia imported a record $8.5 billion worth of food in 2008-09.) It accelerates the increase in urban overcrowding and traffic congestion. It increases Australia's greenhouse emissions, per capita. It makes it unlikely Australia can meet its targets of greenhouse gas emission reduction. It lowers Australia's food security."*

There's no end of similar commentary, including reports supporting immigration that don't let the costs deter them. Overall economic growth due to immigration comes with our per capita economic decline.

"Over the past twenty years, our economic growth has been three point four percent a year," fretted demographer Robert Hall about the economic impact of reducing immigration in 2010, "but if migration falls to the Government's target of a hundred and eighty thousand a year, it would fall to two point seven percent, meaning a big drop in our standard of living." Immigration had just fallen from three hundred and forty-one thousand per year to two hundred and thirty thousand in the year to July 2010 and was likely to continue falling, due to what the government called a natural decline: the global financial crisis. (Financial crises are natural in what we call the natural world.)

Hall saw only the totals, but if the figures he used were correct, then the fall in economic growth overall was an increase in economic growth per person. (At the time, Australia's population was twenty-two million.) The only people suffering a drop in their standard of living might've been demographers.

"*So among business people, economists, and politicians,*" wrote Ross Gittins, economics editor for the *Sydney Morning Herald* newspaper in 2010, "*there is much blind faith in population growth, a belief in growth for its own sake, not because it makes you and me better off.*"

Parliamentary oppositions meekly accede to Western governments admitting more immigrants. When the newly elected Australian government reduced refugee intakes and tightened the rules for conferring welfare benefits upon them and other immigrants from 1996, the Labour Party accused it of abandoning their previous bipartisanship. In 2010, Gittins called bipartisan political support for immigration "*a kind of conspiracy. The nation's business, economic and political elite has always believed in economic growth and, with it, population growth, meaning it has always believed in high immigration.*" The problem was public opinion. "*Hence the tacit decision of the parties to pursue continuing immigration, but not debate it in front of the children.*"

While some scientists argue the country is already close to the limits of the natural environment's "*carrying capacity,*" economists trust undefined technological advances to solve all the problems. "*Business people like high immigration because it gives them an ever-growing market to sell to and profit from,*" wrote Gittins, "*but what's convenient for business is not necessarily good for the economy.*"

Three months later, Gittins played down our focus on economic issues anyway. "*And that's not to say any gain in material standard of living isn't offset by a decline in our quality of life, which goes unmeasured by gross domestic product.*" Immigration costs us no less in social terms than economic ones.

10. IMMIGRATION AND INEQUALITY

Proponents of immigration from my parents' generation, such as my Aunt Anne, claimed countries like Australia and Britain needed immigrants because local people weren't willing to perform particular jobs. Nobody said what those jobs were, but we accepted without question our people wouldn't perform them. For a long time, that was the only reason I heard anyone give as to why we needed immigrants.

Only when writing this book, did I think about that. The people I heard wanting immigrants to perform particular jobs weren't taking such jobs themselves. They employed others, paying tiny wages only immigrants accepted. People who wouldn't sit at a desk for less than a thousand dollars a week complained their compatriots wouldn't clean their bathrooms for a dollar an hour. I'm not sure if any of them asked. Immigration offered them cheap Filipina maids, Chinese gardeners, and Korean house painters.

In 2008, Harvard immigration economist George Borjas said the economic benefits to a nation from immigration "seem much too small" to be worth considering. Immigration being against our national interests doesn't mean it's against everyone's immediate sectional interests. "In the short run, it transfers wealth from one group (workers) to another (employers)."

Without immigration, jobs still got done. We just paid people more money to do them.

Weekend mornings through my last months at college, cleaning lavatories, floors, and other spaces at the Queen's Lynne Nursing Home was probably the worst job I ever had. I wore my worst clothes, secured myself with gloves, and cleaned myself with disinfectant. It was also very well paid, I thought, for that time in my life.

In conducting our business or managing our home, we buy the cheapest acceptable supplies however alien the sources. To the extent labour laws strictly enforced allow, those supplies include people.

When she was in her teens, my wife worked at a McDonald's hamburger restaurant. Having checked she wasn't a member of a trade union, a nearby Chinese restauranteur recruited her from there to waitress in his restaurant too. He paid her cash wages below the award wage and was more demanding than McDonalds. There weren't so many immigrants for hire then, as there are now.

Equality consumes the West, but the racial equality we pursue is between races, not within them. Immigration exacerbates an uneven distribution of incomes, further enriching our rich and impoverishing our poor. Rich and powerful people need a place to belong, but we're satisfied with comfortable big houses behind security gates, clubs with carefully controlled memberships, and anywhere with lawn tennis.

We presume economic growth can be infinite but for the moment, we're confined by finite customers and jobs. Competing for jobs, any immigrant getting a job is at the expense of a compatriot.

Economic analysis in 2009 showed the Australian government's forty-two billion dollar stimulus package wouldn't save the ninety thousand jobs it was supposed to save unless immigration was reduced. Researchers wanted employers to prove local skills weren't available before they imported staff. Not surprisingly, the Australian Industry Group chief executive Heather Ridout condemned the recommendation as a form of economic protectionism (as if that were bad).

"It seems to me that this research could not be right," responded Julia Gillard, then deputy prime minister. No number of reports or studies deters us from our conviction that immigration brings economic benefits.

"*Of jobs created in Texas since 2007,*" said a 2011 report from the Centre for Immigration Studies, "*81 per cent were taken by newly arrived immigrant workers (legal and illegal).*" Legal and illegal immigrants took those jobs in roughly equal numbers. "*This is true even though the native-born accounted for the vast majority of growth in the working-age population (age 16 to 65) in Texas.*"

Not merely the uneducated lose from immigration. "*Immigrants took jobs across the educational distribution. More than one out three (97,000) of newly arrived immigrants who took a job had at least some college.... These numbers raise the question of whether it makes sense to continue the current high level of legal immigration and also whether to continue to tolerate illegal immigration."*

Such results are repeated time and again. In 2014, the centre reported an analysis of Bureau of Labour Statistics data to conclude the net increase in the number of employed working-age adults in North Carolina had gone entirely to legal and illegal immigrants since 2000.

Also in 2014, the centre reported that all America's net employment growth since 2000 had gone to immigrants, legal and illegal. With the American-born population growing, its employment rate fell. The report's authors, Steven Camarota and Karen Zeigler, concluded there never was a general labour shortage and that immigration reduced employment among the American born, as other research had shown.

We're excluding not only our poor but our middle classes not as rich as the richest foreigners. My friend Daven told me in June 2013 of a half-Chinese, half-Persian girl at the prestigious Pymble Ladies College, commenting upon the school shutting out Australians because it wanted Chinese and other Asian money. Daven thought she might've felt a little sad for us.

Unable to comprehend anything but individualism, we've come to attribute our past restrictions on immigration to what Australian Institute of Public Affairs research fellow Chris Berg in 2011 called *"a racist zeitgeist."* (If that was a zeitgeist, then it's still enveloping the rest of the world. Really, the zeitgeist is ours: our new anti-racial zeitgeist.) Berg went onto explain that restricting immigration had been far more practical. *"…the White Australia policy was led by a union movement trying to eliminate competition in the labour market."*

We restricted immigration until the 1960s to protect working white people. Andrew Fisher, Australian Labour Party prime minister through various periods between 1908 and 1915, wanted employers to fire "coloured" workers, according "absolute preference" to white trade unionists.

When socialists cared about white people, the Australian Socialist League was explicit. It called for the "exclusion of races whose presence under present competitive conditions might lower the standard of living of Australian workers."

Berg was scathing. *"Opposition to…outsourcing and labour migration has always been tightly bound up with xenophobia. In Australian history, racism has usually had an economic context… On what moral basis is limiting immigration to protect workers from competition a good thing... Protectionism is bad for many reasons… But its moral core is dark. Surely Australians are no more deserving of jobs than people from China, Japan or Singapore. Economic nationalism implies natives are worth more than foreigners."*

Only the West thinks white people caring for each other requires a dark moral core. Xenophobia includes recognising the harm immigration inflicts not just upon our lives but upon our compatriots' lives too. Empathy and loyalty have become mental illness in the West, as a lack of them isn't.

The only jobs and economic well-being we care about are our individual own. When maximising personal profit's at stake, we'd rather place job advertisements all round the world than aid our unemployed neighbours down another man's road. We bleat about labour shortages to import people to work, leaving governments and charities to feed our poor. In national terms, it's economically inefficient, unsustainable, and immoral. Now, there's a dark moral core.

We understand individual interests so well, but only when we're the individuals. The self-interests of some individuals matter more than others.

Only our immigrants and we are allowed to be selfish, not our compatriots. The immigrants we're welcoming compete not with us, but with our compatriots. Almost all the senior executives with whom I've worked have been Western or Jewish. Sitting comfortably in our executive chairs but still desperate to make some more money, our incomes and lifestyles don't suffer, not yet.

We don't expend time to train our unemployed. "Australia will need an increase of…people with quite specific skills over the next decade to fill some of those gaps…," said Australian Industry Group chief executive Innes Willox in 2014, "and obviously we can train our own, but the quickest stopgap measure is to import skills."

We train everyone else. After the March 2010 board meeting of Golden Cross Resources Limited, the chairman spoke of the New Zealand government training Chileans, Panamanians, Filipinos, and others to be isothermal engineers pursuant to the Colombo Plan since 1950, but without training New Zealanders while he'd been a student. By 2010, Chris said only those foreigners had the skills to manage isothermal energy in New Zealand. The skills shortages by which we supposedly need immigration are of our making.

We talk of labour shortages to justify immigration, but there are no labour shortages and will always be labour shortages. We import a thousand plumbers because we need plumbers. Servicing those plumbers and their families means we need more builders, electricians, teachers, doctors, and so forth. We import the people we need to service those people, and so need more plumbers again. They're much like the immigrants we want to pay taxes to support previous immigrants. Immigration feeds demand for more immigration that will never be mollified: an insatiable beast.

Far from preferring our people, more often than not we prefer the unqualified or inexperienced immigrants because they're cheaper. Treating everyone equally, as we do in the West, the only differences between commodity candidates for a job pertain to price: the fees and wages we pay. Immigrants cost less.

The people who claim that immigration has no impact on wages also claim that reducing immigration will increase the prices we pay because it will increase wages. Immigrants curtail the income expectations of people already employed, compelling local people to match them or be unemployed. Employees thus accept lower salaries and wages, increased working hours, or other diminished working conditions.

The people losing most from immigration aren't just poor white people, but the poor among immigrants already arrived. Children of immigrants grow up with expectations like ours. If we think far enough ahead to worry about that, we know more immigrants with lesser expectations will be ready to come.

In November 2008, the Australian Bureau of Statistics reported the number of immigrant workers approaching two million out of a labour force of more than eleven million. Immigrants don't need to work to assist employers. Pools of unemployed pressure the employed.

In evidence to a House of Lords inquiry into immigration in 2007, supermarket chain Sainsbury's said foreign-born workers were highly motivated with a strong work ethic that rubbed off on British-born staff. It didn't identify, so far as I'm aware, which foreign-born workers they were. They might've been Western.

Immigration also transfers wealth from tenants to landlords. Property owners enjoy rental accommodation crises, while tenants struggle to find places to live and pay more when they do. "The inflow of migration is putting pressure on the housing rental market," said the International Monetary Fund about Sydney in

2008.

Simple economics commands that increases in demand can only pressure prices upward, but housing minister Tanya Plibersek rejected any criticism of immigration. She blamed local elderly people wanting to remain in their homes and divorcees wanting places to live.

Chinese-born Joy Mo moved to Vancouver in 2002. By 2013, she was blaming mainland Chinese for pricing her out of Vancouver's property market.

Immigration is good for the immigrants. If not, they return. Some do. They have the right to decide. We don't.

Immigrants disappointed with their experiences might remain and complain their lives aren't as good as are ours, whereupon we try to ease their distress. We nod sympathetically when they accuse our countrymen of racism and march with them when we can, while we call our compatriots feeling aggrieved by immigration lazy and selfish.

Dealing with immigrants' problems distracts us from dealing with our people's problems. In America, the Occupational Safety and Health Administration made improving the safety and health of immigrant workers a priority after studies by it and the Bureau of Labour Statistics in 2008 reported higher fatal work injury rates among Hispanic or Latino workers than workers overall.

I recall, sometime around about the year 2010, hearing a very earnest young woman on Sydney radio saying the best way to help poor people overseas was to bring them into Australia. I didn't hear her elaborate, but I imagine she meant us educating, employing, housing them, and so forth. The services we provide them are fewer services we provide our poor. The time and money we expend improving their lives we don't spend improving the lives of our own.

We say it's all been worthwhile if the immigrants fare better than they would have fared in their countries of origin. If immigration benefits immigrants more than it costs our compatriots then it improves the lot of the human species overall. It doesn't matter to us that the winners so often aren't Western and the losers so often are. Worrying about that would be economic racism. We think it's fair that immigrants benefit at our compatriots' expense.

We don't even mind if our compatriots lose more socially and economically than the immigrants gain, so the human lot is worse overall. We cherish interracial equality more than we want our race to be rich or our poor to be coping.

In our globalist vision, impoverished immigrants are just another facet of global impoverishment. Canadian journalist Doug Saunders, author of *Arrival City: How the Largest Migration in History is Reshaping Our World*, equated immigration overwhelming Western cities with urbanisation outside the West. "That's a universal of bottom-rung immigrant neighbourhoods, whether it's the slums of Mumbai or the suburbs of Sydney," he said in 2011. "A lot of the things that government can do are not so much about spending money, although I argue that some things do need to have money spent on them, but a lot of them are simply a matter of removing impediments to success, getting out of the way, not controlling zoning and housing access, making sure that new immigrants, whether they are documented or not, can start businesses, pay taxes, can buy their housing."

Wildly confident in the merit of immigrants, Saunders blamed immigrants' impoverishment upon our failures to provide for them, as well as business and building regulation. His economic liberty was anarchy, where countries once were. With such determination to remove all roles for regulation, little wonder he didn't care whether immigrants were legally in the country.

Western borders become more pesky regulations. In 2010, Australian National University demographer Peter McDonald argued that governments should leave levels of net immigration to economic forces. Economic recession deterred immigrants and more local people left. Economic booms had the reverse effect. He would remove all roles for government in controlling borders, dismantling our countries altogether.

What's good for some immigrant races is bad for those unwilling to join a subservient underclass. Professor Darrell Hamamoto warned in June 2014 that the University of California was preparing for what it called "Hispanisation." He called illegal immigration a deliberate plan "to exclude the American middle class from a U.C. education and create a new demographic of largely immigrant or foreign national undergraduate population that can be re-educated from the ground up and controlled much more readily."

11. INDIVIDUALISM AND IMMIGRATION

Nationalism is compatriots caring for each other. Individualism is people caring only for themselves, and perhaps people close to them.

One explanation as to why Britain and France opened their borders to their former colonial possessions in numbers we'd never previously imagined was gratitude to soldiers who'd helped defend them during World War II, but any gratitude wasn't limited to those who'd fought. Besides, thousands of Indians had volunteered for the German Army's *Legion Freies Indien* and the Italian Army, including some prisoners of war who'd formerly fought with the British.

We also allowed other races to come. Western countries that hadn't led empires or fought in the war unilaterally opened their borders too.

Hans was a tall thin blond-haired larrikin of a man, who'd abandoned the high taxation rates of his native Sweden to reside in Andorra. When I met him in Western Samoa late in 1987, he was travelling the South Pacific trying to sell power stations generating electricity from waves. The recent murder of Sweden's Prime Minister Olof Palme neither surprised nor concerned him. After all, said Hans, "He was a socialist."

Hans went onto explain that Palme opened Sweden to Kurds to help Palme's personal ambition to become head of the United Nations: a private world empire. Without nationalism, we see not just our countries but also the world in terms of our acutely individual interests. The West remains an age of empires, in which national empires gave way to individual, egocentric empires. Countries are no more than means for individuals to exploit. So is the world. Ours are the empires of one.

The only life Palme cared about was his own. Hans cared no more about Palme's life than Palme had cared about Hans', while Palme presumed he could continue to walk unprotected with his wife through the streets of Stockholm at night. The murder remains unsolved, but Hans implied that if his killer was a Kurd that Palme's global ambition allowed into Sweden, then his murder would have been more than merely ironic. It would have been justice.

Western individualism gave rise to multiracial immigration. Multiculturalism exacerbates our individualism.

Trade union leaders embraced interracial immigration for the same rejection of race and country as did other Western leaders, but racial diversity broke down much of our collective trade union culture, to the great glee of employers. While studying Law and driving taxis, my friend Philip wanted to unionise the taxi drivers to improve their income and working conditions. Indian drivers thwarted him. Not only had they no affinity for Australians, they didn't want to draw attention to their work driving taxis in violation of the student visas by which Australia allowed them to come.

We're passing through diversity into Asianisation. To talk of Australia's Asianisation had been regarded as xenophobic. By 2012, not talking about it was xenophobic.

The Sydney Morning Herald newspaper eagerly reported the 2011 census proving the "*accelerating Asianisation of a country built on the xenophobia of white Australia…*" Any defence of country by white people is xenophobia.

We're much like America, where talk of Latinisation and Hispanisation is positively progressive. We're well ahead of our kin left in Europe, where talk of Islamisation is still xenophobic.

What we're really enthusing for is the solitary chasm of individualism. "*As affiliations wilted,*" said *The Sydney Morning Herald*, "*as social mobility and broadening of education raised aspiration and expectation, the shibboleths tumbled, loosening the grip of the collective and trumpeting the individual.*"

Our education and social mobility narrowed. Those of other races grew. They've retained their affiliations. We've become more individualistic.

We venerate individualism and Asianisation, but there's no individualism in Asia. We've become intrinsically individuals, while the country becomes Asian. None of it makes sense, but we're no longer much good at making sense. We're just doing our darnedest not to be a nation or race. At its core, individualism is about us: each of us white people separating ourselves from each other. Each individual's triumph is his or her race's defeat.

Asianisation isn't globalisation, nor is Latinisation or Islamisation. What was a bloc of Western civilisation across Europe, the Americas, and Australasia becomes bits of other people's blocs.

We don't have a bloc anymore. We're individuals. Our individualism allows other races' expansion.

As is often the case whenever white people purport to speak of national identities, parliamentarian Lindsay Tanner could've been speaking about any number of Western countries in his Redmond Barry Lecture of 2008. The author of *Open Australia*, Tanner equated open borders with other openness, as only we in recent years would. Central to our new, post-national identities is not being nations at all.

"We don't all adhere collectively to a defined set of values," said Tanner, of the country in which he was born. "We harbour many different senses of Australian identity... There are some things, however, that I think are deeply embedded in our collective spirit. There is a sense of openness, energy and decency that is a very distinctive feature of the Australian character. Other words like fairness, tolerance, and enterprise could be added, but I think openness, energy and decency are the words that best reflect who and what we are." Identity had become a matter of values.

Asia was heavy with open, energetic peoples, but presumably lacked our senses of decency. Tanner never explained how immigrants arrive and suddenly share his collective spirit, but they don't need to. As always, immigration is about us. "This issue is about how we see ourselves," said Tanner, "and how we see new arrivals in our community."

We see ourselves as individuals decent to other races, separated from our own. Those other races see themselves as peoples.

Tanner listed African success stories. They were all Africans focused upon their communities or acting as individuals outside them.

The onus is on us to help the newcomers, as it isn't on us helping each other or on the immigrants being responsible for themselves. "We have to make an effort," said Tanner, "not just sit back and allow them to sink or swim. If we do, the rewards for all of us will be overwhelming." Tanner never specified those rewards, unless he meant employing them. "Aged-care facilities now employ numerous African Australian nurses," he said, although I'd heard anecdotally about those Africans failing to attend and performing poorly when they did.

I suspect the rewards Tanner contemplated are simply white people feeling proud of ourselves, hidden somewhere in our heads. Immigration involves not just our willingness to give up our countries, but our enthusiasm for doing so. We're not so generous with our meagre houses and apartments, as we are with countries we don't want anyway.

If we're not in denial about the impact of interracial immigration upon our races and countries, it's because we don't care. All our compatriots can lose from the whole immigration process provided we think we gain personally, however little our gain happens to be. We don't even need to gain, provided we think we don't personally lose.

We do lose. Indiscriminate immigration undermines the economic structures that help us carry on business. Africans hawk crappy leather handbags from footpaths throughout Italy to a degree we don't want to do, but only xenophobic shopkeepers selling handbags would complain. It's de facto deregulation.

In court for an unrelated matter in the late 1980s, I observed another East Asian fisherman fined for using illegal nets to catch undersized fish. We good hosts and hostesses blamed the immigrants' ignorance of local laws and their misunderstanding of local language, but they knew the laws and local language enough.

Vietnamese refugees (trained in French cooking) and other immigrants repeatedly broke restrictions upon Sydney bakeries operating on Sundays. The restrictions fell apart.

Our local shopping precinct was a pretty, quaint place, with long wooden benches and bright flowers, trees, and green hedges along the footpaths. For thirty years, the only barber was Frank, but late in 2007, a gangly Vietnamese man set up a second barbershop nearby. His name, I learned almost a year later from Bill at our parish Anglican church, was Thanh.

Thanh's shop was bright and modern, almost garish, with bright lights and pictures, clean walls, and no sporting memorabilia in sight. Within days of his opening, perhaps even before he opened, Thanh noticed me pausing to read the notice in his shop window. He quickly bundled after my children and me into the adjoining Pizza Hut store and, without speaking words I understood and still recall, thrust his advertising flyer into my hand.

The local council restricted street-side advertising to maintain the beauty of that small local precinct, but Thanh affixed ugly handwritten posters advertising his barbershop to fences, telegraph poles, and the wall by the exit to a shopping centre car park. There was hardly an open space on which the thick black text of his handwriting on white or bright yellow cardboard didn't appear. Presumably more expense went into the ugly huge printed banners covering his van, which he parked in the commuter car park by the railway station, in other car parks, and at kerbs throughout our suburb and adjoining suburbs. I'm sure everyone presumed and accepted his ignorance of local council by-laws.

The flyer Thanh gave me in the pizza shop, like some of his posters and banners, promised a thirty percent discount in the first two weeks he was open. Thus that New Year's Eve, I took my three young sons there for haircuts. Perhaps Frank's was closed that day. Perhaps I wanted to give the new arrival a chance. Most importantly, the thirty percent discount was attractive with four haircuts to buy, but his arithmetic no better than his English reduced men's haircuts from eighteen to fifteen dollars and boys' haircuts from fifteen to thirteen dollars.

Good Australians would have presumed and accepted his arithmetic errors. I wasn't so good. We left without him cutting our hair.

Thanh's ubiquitous advertising continued, without regard for neighbourhood aesthetics. Eight months after his barbershop opened, his huge black felt pen scrawled poster was affixed, close to our local railway station, to the side of a charity bin collecting clothes for the poor.

Bill laughed; Bill laughed a lot. We've become relentless businesspeople too.

Thanh's barbershop was open seven days a week, until late every day. Frank's barbershop closed Saturday afternoons and Sundays. Economic extremists like the stress and competition intrinsic to multiculturalism, thinking we thrive under pressure, but we've lost some chance to relax. Frank was too generous to complain, but if his barbershop (since he passed away) has to open every day to survive, then his son and other barbers lose their choice to live any other way.

The third Saturday in March 2010, my friend Namoi lamented

the poverty of Britain's underclass abandoned by the Labour Party government in power for the past fourteen years. I'd never seen their sorry lives on the television news, but she'd recently been to Britain and seen it. The years have left people poorer, without a country to care.

The following Friday, sitting on the platform at our local railway station was a wreck of a man. His clothes and hair even more ragged than he was made him seem old, but his skin wasn't old. In his twenties, he was younger than I was: I in my dark pinstriped suit. He was alone, not begging, as if he'd learnt not to bother.

Another man of his age, poorly dressed but not ragged, boarded the train I boarded. Soon, he and another man of their age and appearance were swearing at each other. Loud and boorish but not menacing, they staggered about. The first man swore at the other for making so much noise, while he was trying to speak on a mobile telephone. (No matter how poor or wretched people are, they still have mobile telephones.) When one came upstairs in the carriage and slumped in a seat near me, I saw words in white printed on his black tee shirt: "*Do something useful with your life, get me a beer!*"

People wealthier than they were boarded the train, including so many Asians at Chatswood. Nobody cared about the wretched Australians. So proudly have we abandoned nationalism, we care nothing for our countries that no longer exist or the people who could've been our compatriots. We don't think of us having compatriots at all.

Asian countries had become wealthy and used their wealth to help their races. We too help their poor.

We could have done so much with our wealth to help our poor, but we neglect them. Our poor aren't studying or working as the immigrants study and work. They have their payments of welfare, but few people encouraging them to free themselves from dependence. They aren't building lives or creating arts but are awfully alone, stumbling about.

Walking from Town Hall railway station, another friendless white man faced me. "Can I have some dollars for a train fare?" he asked, his voice weak and absent.

"No," I replied, without breaking stride.

I'd often visited George Street as a child to see films in the cinema precinct, without seeing beggars or paupers. Nor had I then been a racial minority.

At forty-eight years of age, I was headed to the city offices of a major accountancy firm: the auditors for Golden Cross Resources Limited. Scores of employees and clients heard presentations about financial reporting and transactions in the resources industries from experts like Mike (a partner I think from the firm's assurance and advisory business services section) speaking dispassionately about China's expansion. *"China has state backing exceeding $2t in reserves,"* said one page of the presentation displayed before the audience, *"and a supportive 'go out' policy."*

That complimented the West, I thought to myself. We have a supportive "come in" policy.

I think Mike was again speaking a short time later when the page presented began: *"What's headed – a new era."* The first point below it stated: *"A shift from west to east and north to south."* The ideas had often been spoken and written about, but what struck me was the speaker's complete indifference to the decline of the countries and race of which he was a part. He could've been describing ants in a hill.

So much the individuals, those of us who don't revel in our downfall, just observe. We remark and prepare presentations to audiences more interested in the tea or coffee at the break coming soon.

At afternoon's end, I drank glasses of wine and ate canapés served by Asian waiters, standing in soon-forgotten conversations with Asian and other accountants. Confident our wealth will shield us from what happens to others, we might move readily elsewhere, or die before very much deteriorates. Among the streets somewhere below, trumpeted white individuals languished in raggedy clothes.

12. REFUGEES
AND OUR NOBLESSE OBLIGE

For those of us most able to help others, we have Europe's traditional noblesse oblige: our moral duty to attend plush dinners and cocktail parties to aid the fashionably unfortunate. Noblemen and women helped our poor who couldn't help but be poor, before widening that to the poor of all Europe.

Europe and her colonies granted refuge for Europeans and Jews evading religious persecution because we chose to grant it, suffering no harm because of it. Protestant and Roman Catholic countries gave refuge to small numbers of fellow Europeans of their religion fleeing the other. They were immigrants, at a time immigration was rare.

Through the 1930s, Britain accepted Jews fleeing Nazism, including the founder of psychiatry Sigmund Freud after Germany invaded Austria in March 1938. Freud's home in Hampstead was a beautiful big mansion, with a restful space of soft chairs on a small landing halfway up the front stairs. Australia accepted a Hungarian Jew who earned a fortune importing rugs from China. In time, he became my Uncle Paul.

Unfolding was a new class of people we called refugees. In July 1938, America's President Franklin Delano Roosevelt convened a meeting with European countries, Australia, and some Latin American countries in Evian-les-Bains to discuss "The Organization of the Emigration and Resettlement" of "Political Refugees and Those Persecuted by Reason of Race or Religion." At the conference, Germany and Austria eased slightly their exit procedures for Jews, allowing some of them to take portions of their possessions.

A few Latin American countries accorded entry visas to small numbers of Jews. Only two countries outside Europe agreed to accept significant numbers. Australia undertook to grant fifteen thousand entry permits over three years. Unlike other European colonies, Jews had always been with the British in Australia: eight of them had been convicts aboard the First Fleet. The Dominican Republic undertook unconditionally to receive up to a hundred thousand Jews.

(That didn't mean the Dominican Republic was forever open to all. In 2015, the Dominican government pledged to deport foreign citizens, primarily black Haitians, who didn't submit applications to establish legal residency before the last Wednesday in June.)

Zionist leader Chaim Weizmann, who went onto become the first Israeli president in 1949, wasn't satisfied. Wrong as he was, he saw an anti-Semitic world in the 1930s divided into "two factions: one formed by the countries that are expelling the Jews and the other formed by those who refuse to admit them."

The 1974 book and 1976 film *Voyage of the Damned* were inspired by the German ocean liner M.S. *St Louis*, which set forth from Hamburg to Cuba in May 1939 carrying more than nine hundred Jews. Twenty-two of them left the ship in Cuba, before America and Canada refused the rest entry. Britain, Belgium, France, and the Netherlands accepted them, but Nazi Germany would soon occupy the latter three. Historians estimate that more than two hundred *St Louis* Jews died during the war. They would have survived had Cuba, America, or Canada taken them (but also if they'd gone to the Dominican Republic).

Their deaths led to the United Nations Convention Relating to the Status of Refugees in 1951, which the signatories envisaged applying only to Europeans and Jews fleeing Soviet communism. (Seeing a group of them in free Nuremberg 1986 mulling senselessly around a lake, I knew there was no other reason to take them.) The refugee convention was a Cold War response to communism as much as the Holocaust.

A decade later, America accepted Cubans fleeing the communist revolution in Cuba. They were largely upper-class white.

"The only things I hate are want, misery, and insecurity of any people in any country," said Ben Chifley, who became Australian prime minister in 1945. The mood was to populate or we'd perish, and Chifley's government opened the country to all Europeans. With Britain so weakened by a second world war, a European Australia was more likely than British Australia to survive another threat from Asia.

The refuge we'd generously granted tens of thousands of

Chinese, Indochinese, and Malayan wartime refugees was only for the course of the war. After Japan's defeat in 1945, their case for refuge ended. Australia deported them, including some who'd married Australian citizens and were raising families, back to their homelands. "I have no racial animosity," immigration minister Arthur Calwell (a policeman's son) told the Australian parliament on the sixth day of October 1948. He counted many Chinese among his friends, going so far as to learn Mandarin to converse with them. The White Australia Policy remained intact.

As minister for the army from 1966 until '68, wealthy grazier Malcolm Fraser oversaw the conscription of young Australians to fight and die for Vietnam in the Vietnamese War. From 1969 until '71 (when his resignation from the ministry brought down John Gorton's government), Fraser oversaw the conduct of the war as minister for defence. As Liberal Party leader in 1975, Fraser wielded his coalition's senate majority to block the supply of money to the Australian government, bringing the country to her knees. No other politician in Australian history betrayed so many people and caused so many traumas in pursuit of personal power.

Becoming prime minister, Fraser proudly declared Australia's immigration policies to be "colour-blind." Having failed to save Vietnam for the Vietnamese, in spite of our young men he sacrificed, Fraser gave them our country instead. Only with the end of the Vietnam War in 1975 did the West start accepting substantial numbers of refugees from other races permanently. No longer do we grant refuge only for as long as refugees need it, and provided our people aren't harmed.

Fraser considered himself heroic, helping hopeless races within his paternalistic power and grace to control. Charity to white people, Fraser would have considered unimaginable humility. Completely uninterested in our wants, Fraser infamously fended off working-class Australians with the phrase, "Life isn't meant to be easy."

He'd corrupted the quote from Irish playwright George Bernard Shaw in *Back to Methuselah (A Metabiological Pentateuch)* without completing it. *"Life is not meant to be easy, my child; but take courage: it can be delightful."* It became delightful for the Vietnamese.

Fraser's miseries mattered, nobody else's. He cried when he lost the 1983 election to Bob Hawke.

Tears often filled Hawke's eyes. He cried for his daughter

Rosslyn's problems with heroin. In June 1989, he wept for Chinese demonstrators wanting democracy dispersed from Tiananmen Square, Beijing, with apparently hundreds of fatalities. The Australian Labour Party no longer supported Australian labour or Australia (except in sport). At a tearful whim, Hawke created a new category of immigrant to allow fifty thousand Chinese students and others to remain in Australia because they happened to be here at the time.

The fifty thousand Chinese weren't fleeing anything. Far from being persecuted, their families would've been wealthy and politically well-connected for them to be overseas. They might well have supported the Chinese government crackdown.

Following the Chinese government crackdown, I walked with a protest march in Sydney for a block or two, headed in the direction I was headed anyway. Later that year, at the Ku-ring-gai Municipal Council Christmas party, I confronted the Chinese consul in Sydney. "What I thought you did was disgusting," I told him.

I came to regret my rudeness, realising I'd been swept up in our postmodern imperialism. When I learnt to believe in countries again, I realised the events in Beijing were matters for China and the Chinese. They were none of my business.

Twenty-six years afterwards, a Chinese-born Australian senator, Zhenya Wang, defended the Tiananmen Square massacre as "the right thing to do." Otherwise, China "would have descended into hell."

I shouldn't have worried about other people's countries. I should've worried about mine.

Refugees had become the principal objects of our postmodern affection: the West's cause célèbre, our global noblesse oblige. The most treacherous of illegal immigrants command our sympathies by claiming asylum, with all the rights and trust the West grants them.

Had we thought during World War II as we think now, Japan would've never needed to contemplate invading Australia. Japanese ships would've needed only to reach Australian territorial waters laden with Japanese soldiers who then claimed asylum. (Japan could also have shut down the American fleet at Pearl Harbour by calling it culturally insensitive.)

Title determined traditional nobility. Politics and money determine our postmodern nobility. They determine pretty well everything in our commercial, political West.

Our money-made nobility needn't be particularly rich to offer cash as much as our causes. Our middle-class neighbourhoods form refugee welcome committees, standing ready to drape cloths over tables and cut cucumber sandwiches. We'll welcome anyone telling us how awful is the rest of the world and how glad they are to have come.

Ku-ring-gai Council joined other Western local councils to declare the municipality a Refugee Welcome Zone. They're not referring to refugees from other municipalities and shires, where the houses and gardens aren't so nice. (I know. I used to live in one.) They're not even referring to the suburbs where houses are positively awful, without a geranium in sight. No, they're referring to any faraway foreigners claiming refugee status, or even the black man loitering about our local railway station a few days before I wrote those words.

There will never be solutions to other countries' problems while we admit the people who could solve them. If we think circumstances are so dire or oppressive elsewhere that justice or mercy demands we admit refugees, then it begs us to aid and protect people they've left behind. The logical consequence of granting asylum is a willingness to replace tyrannical or incompetent regimes in other countries, but we're not willing to intervene: to return to empire. Granting refuge is a weak, lazy response.

Most illegal immigrants reaching the West have passed through several countries along the way, but asylum in the West is a much better offer. Indonesia let fellow Muslims enjoy their lives there in August 2001, when more than four hundred Afghans tried to sneak their way into Australia aboard a twenty-metre-long boat. Approximately a hundred and fifty kilometres from the Australian territory of Christmas Island, the boat sounded distress. A Norwegian ship the M.V. *Tampa* diverted her journey to bring them aboard. They promptly claimed refugee status.

The *Tampa* headed towards the Indonesian ferry port of Merak, but the Afghans hadn't travelled so far or paid so much money to people smugglers to go back to where they'd spent long enough already. A delegation of five Afghans went to the Norwegian captain and aggressively demanded they be taken to Christmas Island. The captain meekly complied.

The Australian government wasn't so compliant, refusing the illegal immigrants entry to Christmas Island. Never before in my memory had a Western government so publicly turned away so many illegal immigrants claiming refugee status. The *Tampa* quickly became the hottest political issue of my adult life, dominating not just the media but popular conversation. As I walked through Sydney's prestigious David Jones department store, I overheard two women tending to the counters talking about it.

Among the scores of shoppers when the immigration minister Philip Ruddock entered the Bunnings hardware store in Thornleigh was Carl, the part-time accountant at Golden Cross Resources Limited. With the minister were two bodyguards, protecting him from people who would assault or kill him because the government was denying entry to the Afghans. Instead of trying to harm him that day, the shoppers broke into applause. The first to applaud might've been uncommonly brave, or felt emboldened by the government. Eight years later, in a conversation about the popular Ruddock, Carl told me about it.

Critics accused the Australian government of blaming the country's problems upon the influx of relatively small numbers of asylum seekers, without explaining what those problems were. They were economic good times, so the economy wasn't a problem. They might've been thinking about social problems, but refusing to consider a link between race and crime denied critics much chance to proceed with that one.

They accused the government of being populist (as if that were bad) and politically opportunistic (as if governments weren't). They're common criticisms of any suggestion Western governments curtail immigration or restrict the benefits given immigrants. The accusation acknowledges that's what people want.

Critics claimed that turning the *Tampa* away (and detaining asylum seekers who reached Australia) harmed Australia's relationship with Asian countries. New South Wales premier Bob Carr (whose wife was Malaysian) asked the Singaporean deputy prime minister how Singapore treated asylum seekers. "We arrest them," the Singaporean replied, "we cane them, we keep them in jail and we send them back to where they came from." They didn't cease being illegal immigrants by claiming asylum.

The only harm from not letting the *Tampa* unload the Afghans in Australia was in our relations with other Western countries.

Aside from United Nations commissioners, we're the people most pressing each other to take more immigrants and who think less of us when we don't. *"The 460 refugees on board MV Tampa dreamed of an idyllic life overlooking Sydney Harbour,"* lamented the *Observer* newspaper in London, trusting the asylum seekers to be refugees. *"Now, thanks to global inaction and Australian domestic politics, they could end up on a pile of seagull droppings. If they're lucky."*

The pile of seagull droppings was the island republic of Nauru to which the Afghans were initially sent, and where more than ten thousand Nauruans lived freely. It was all positively welcoming compared to anything on offer from rich Asian countries.

The most compelling observation I read or heard through that time credited the government's soaring popularity among Australians to a sense that, rarely in our postmodern West, a government stood up for the country it governed. We'd long stopped expecting Western governments to side with us, but for those few days and weeks, Australians had a moment of country. We thought being Australian meant something.

We were wrong. The government continued insisting it (instead of aspiring immigrants and United Nations agencies) controlled Australia's borders, deciding the people the country admitted and the terms on which they came, but quietly continued admitting huge numbers of Asian and African refugees and other immigrants. We just didn't admit them by boat. Most of the Afghans from the *Tampa* ended up in New Zealand and a hundred or so in Australia anyway. For every Afghan from the *Tampa* who didn't, another Asian or African came from elsewhere by reason of Australia's willingness to accept set numbers of thousands of refugees.

The government's response had been a lie. We weren't controlling our borders, but ushering immigrants through another ingress.

Refugee advocates weren't interested in the reality. The rhetoric so appealing to some remained galling to many.

At his Bradfield electorate conference endorsement meeting in 2007, Brendan Nelson told the story of a woman before the 2004 Australian election. Doubtlessly proud of what she'd have seen as her grand social conscience, she'd almost certainly never encountered an asylum seeker and almost certainly never would, not in the affluent northern suburbs of Sydney in which she lived, played, and dined. Dressed for her tennis club and drinking

Champagne, she told a journalist she would vote against the government because it wasn't welcoming refugees.

The journalist asked her if she was concerned about the impact a change in government could have on the Australian economy. An economic downturn could harm the lives of millions of other Australians.

Her charity wasn't to white people, while feasting on Champagne and *Tampa*. If she encountered poor Australians in her comfortable rich life, waiting on her table or cleaning her car, she probably didn't notice them. We're so kind to strangers, applauding ourselves that we are, but not to people we meet. "Why should *I* care about the economy?" she asked the journalist. "*My* husband earns six hundred thousand dollars a year."

13. AN IDEOLOGY
CALLED COMPASSION

We used to have national rights and personal obligations: a place in the world. We now have personal rights and national obligations: all alone in the world.

We have none of the national rights other races enjoy. The only times we talk of nations, Western nations at any rate, are in the context of our supposed duties to others: our parting gestures before disappearing altogether. Only the West resettles refugees from other races and cultures, but we feel no pride for it. We take not personal but collective responsibility: rarely countenancing individual obligations, at least upon us, while suffering national obligations aplenty.

During a visit to Italy in 2010, Libyan dictator Muammar Gaddafi warned Europe would turn "black" if she didn't turn back immigrants. "We don't know if Europe will remain an advanced and united continent or if it will be destroyed, as happened with the barbarian invasions."

Unwilling to assert her borders herself, the West's straitjacket of rights we grant foreigners meant Italy paid Gaddafi five billion euros a year to hold back illegal migration from Africa through Libya to Europe. Like lawful immigration, unlawful immigration creates opportunities for the rest of the world. Gaddafi lost power in 2011.

In 2012, the European Court of Human Rights ruled that Italy couldn't return illegal immigrants she'd picked up adrift in the Mediterranean Sea to Libya. "Even on the high seas," said Judith Sunderland, senior Western Europe researcher at Human Rights Watch, "European states can't wash their hands of responsibilities towards migrants and refugees." At a time Italy was struggling to rein in government expenses and stave off economic recession, she had to pay twenty-two Somalis and Eritreans fifteen thousand euros each.

Our obligations don't end with admitting them. Granting refuge isn't enough.

Sudanese refugee Ayan Majok moved into Melbourne suburban Laverton in 2008 with her husband and five children. A year later, fellow refugee Hawa Mahmoud, her husband, and seven children moved in next door. "We don't have a park for the kids to go and play in," complained Majok, although the street was a Sudanese playground. "There's no school around here, no shops around here, no petrol station and now we have a bus, but not many services. If you don't have a car or the car breaks down, you have to walk twenty-five or thirty minutes to the shop."

Other residents like Shawn Lynch also complained that the Victorian government wasn't doing more, although we expect less from our governments than immigrants do. The state was suffering what the *Age* newspaper called Victoria's population explosion, due to immigration.

In 2010, Anglicare Sydney chief executive Peter Kell wasn't concerned about Australians renting rundown houses or being homeless as much as he was about Sudanese refugees unsatisfied with their rental houses; poor darlings. "They've come here with great expectations of starting a new life in a new country," said Kell, "and yet they're telling us that it's not working for them."

Our obligations to refugees weren't just to give them refuge, money, healthcare, education, and a house. We had to give them a house that they liked, where they liked. While we're uninterested in living with our race, we've great respect for people of other races wanting to live with theirs, but the Sudanese couldn't afford to live in suburbs with established African communities, such as Granville and Mount Druitt. Kell wanted real estate agents to help Sudanese and the New South Wales government to build them more housing.

Accepting refugees is expensive. The expense never ends.

Multicultural Sudanese Centre manager Elhadi Abass blamed three nights of violence by Sudanese in Melbourne in April 2011 not upon the Sudanese, but upon a lack of funding for programmes focussed upon young Sudanese men. "We are trying to get through to them, but we have no budget," he complained. "We find ourselves asking, 'How will the state government help us?'"

Australian governments already provided refugees with six months' training for employment, but still African Think Tank head Berhan Ahmed blamed the violence on Australia's humanitarian assistance "stopping at the airport" and not training Africans to find jobs and engage with others. "It's all been meeting and meeting and meeting," he complained. "For the last four or five years, we've been meeting."

Ahmed seemed to have done rather well. Born in Eritrea before reaching a refugee camp in Sudan, the United Nations High Commission for Refugees funded his schooling. He came to Australia as a refugee in the late 1980s. "We should have been ambassadors of change and acceptance for blackness," he said. "The system still has a problem accepting that blackness...and that's what's halting Africans in their settlement." He accused us of a history of failure on blackness (despite naming him Victorian of the Year in 2009).

In Sydney, the onus was upon us to stop an Afghan faction within the Brothers for Life gang carrying out the bloodiest gun violence through 2013. Its thirty-year-old leader's family had sought asylum in Australia and beaten three murder charges through the past four years.

"This is a whole of society problem," claimed New South Wales deputy police commissioner Nick Kaldas, insisting the series of brazen murders, kidnappings, extortions, and other crimes were about profit, not race or Islam. (We understand money better than we understand race or culture.) "There are issues with disadvantage, there are issues with a whole lot of anger in youth, all of that stuff police cannot fix on their own."

Former New South Wales assistant police commissioner Clive Small also blamed us for refugee crime, because we'd not given them more. "What we've seen with Australia's immigration history is very much the case that when you have large intakes of refugees coming to Australia, particularly where they don't speak English... they're not given the support they need to mix with Australia in terms of competing for jobs, employment, understanding the language, and so they become a disadvantaged group," he said. "That disadvantage pushes the young kids into gangs."

Many refugees are very advantaged. For fear of offending Saudi Arabia, Britain kept quiet a British court granting asylum to a Saudi princess in 2009. Her adultery made her liable to flogging and stoning to death under sharia. (Presumably that wasn't an aspect of sharia the British were considering adopting to accommodate

Britain's growing Muslim population.)

We acknowledge the offence to our allies that granting refugee status to their citizens can cause, if they don't realise what a free-for-all the refugee industry is, but still grant it. We just don't mention it.

Much had changed in South Africa by 2009, when the Canadian Immigration and Refugee Board granted asylum to Brandon Huntley because he'd been racially persecuted in South Africa and would likely be again if he returned there. What made the case interesting was that Huntley was white. Seven times, black assailants in South Africa attacked him, calling him a "white dog" and a "settler." Three times they stabbed him. The black South African government wasn't protecting white people from violence.

While Huntley was proud to have drawn attention to reality in South Africa since apartheid ended, Huntley's estranged Canadian wife Melanie Crete-Huntley objected to him disrespecting black South Africa. A hundred and thirty-three academics from thirteen South African and six overseas universities wrote a public letter to Canada's chargé d'affaires in Pretoria, Jeff White, rejecting Huntley's claims. The ruling African National Congress called his claims "sensational and alarming," saying "Canada's reasoning for granting Huntley a refugee status can only serve to perpetuate racism."

Accusing black people of racism is racist. Granting white people refuge from that racism would compound it.

The Canadian Department of Citizenship and Immigration appealed the board's decision to the Canadian Federal Court. It overturned the decision in 2010 partly because Huntley had spent time in Canada before seeking asylum.

There are some limits upon being postmodern refugees. They can't be white.

Beyond that, limits are few. In September 2012, the Australian Department of Immigration and Citizenship gave a bridging visa to a Sri Lankan asylum seeker accused of murdering his girlfriend in Sri Lanka. The department cancelled that visa in April 2013, the same month the media reported an Egyptian asylum seeker in the Inverbrackie detention centre in the Adelaide Hills was the subject of an Interpol red notice and accused of terrorism. The department transferred him only so far as Villawood in Sydney.

Drug trafficking charges didn't deter the department from

bringing an Iranian asylum seeker from Nauru to Australia and a mental health hospital. "He's being treated for his illness," explained department secretary Martin Bowles in May. "He's quite ill."

The Netherlands granted Somali-born Ayaan Hirsi Ali refuge in 1992. By 2010, she was arguing the 1951 refugee convention was obsolete, unable to deal with large numbers of immigrants. "This convention is from a different era," she pointed out. "It doesn't work for our time."

The convention is a Cold War relic. The end of East European communism in 1989 and '91 made it obsolete, if it wasn't already.

Refugee claims, said Hirsi Ali, should be rigorously assessed on the applicant's ability to contribute to the host nation. "So what I am trying to say is that we have to change the paradigm. You have to say, 'You're welcome, we need immigrants but there are many conditions. Here is the law, the culture, the customs. Here is what you agree to, and in exchange you get to live in a peaceful, prosperous society where you have all this opportunity. If you don't agree we will just return you'."

In effect, Hirsi Ali called for ending the refugee regime as a distinct category of immigration. She said it's futile for Western countries to try to establish the bona fides of asylum seekers, not least because they say anything to qualify for asylum. "Everybody lies," she said.

She'd obtained asylum by telling Dutch authorities she was fleeing the war in Somalia. In fact, she was escaping a marriage arranged by her father.

We're uninterested in facts that don't accord with our convictions we're compassionate. We insist asylum seekers are telling the truth as if questioning them was a flaw, although their applications to immigrate depend on their answers. We confuse justice with trust, believing whatever other races say to claim our compassion.

Nafissatou Diallo told a moving story of being gang raped in Guinea to obtain asylum in America. She repeated the story to New York prosecutors after alleging International Monetary Fund chief Dominique Strauss-Kahn raped her in his room at the Manhattan Sofitel Hotel in 2011, speaking with so much emotion that "she cried, spoke hesitatingly, and... even laid her head face down on a table in front of her."

She lied. Her story of the rape in Guinea was a lie. In spite of other evidence Strauss-Khan had assaulted her, Diallo's record of lies led prosecutors to abandon their prosecution of him. So convincing a lie she'd repeated about one sexual assault would allow his lawyers to argue she was lying about another.

Instead of reasons for people to be truthful, we create reasons for them to lie, manipulating us. "My work on the Migration Review Tribunal has taught me that people are all the same," said my friend Namoi. She meant it so nicely, but people aren't all as noble as she is.

Her words exuded a truth different to the truth she intended. Without reason to be truthful, people say whatever they think helps them get what they want. White people do. Other races lie to enter the West, but if we could fly back through time to 1939, we wouldn't refuse Jews fleeing Nazism for being liars.

From its earliest days, the 1951 refugee convention facilitated liars and cheats. Hungarian wrestler Steve Raskovy fled Hungary after the communist Soviet Union crushed the Hungarian uprising in 1956. Among the Hungarians on his ship to Australia was a large proportion of Hungarian-speaking Romanians, lying their way.

Raskovy's refugee experiences taught him to secure Western borders. Fifty-three years later, he was a candidate in the by-election for the federal electorate of Higgins, covering a wealthy and privileged part of Melbourne. Among other things, he wanted cuts to immigration and the forced repatriation of illegal immigrants.

More than sixty-six thousand votes were validly cast at that 2009 by-election. Raskovy received two hundred and eleven. The Sex Party candidate, Fiona Patten, received more than two thousand.

Individualism is as central to the West resettling refugees from other races as it is to the rest of our indiscriminate immigration. Every right we give others comes with a cost (even if paid to lawyers), but we think we only suffer what we suffer individually. Thinking we lose nothing whoever might come, we care nothing for our ignoble compatriots struggling to deal with their declining lives, provided we hold true to our individual selves. In the height of our selective compassion, we'll believe every story of suffering from someone seeking asylum, but not bother with testimony from victims of crimes refugees commit.

Safely secure in our tucked-away homes, we sit snug in our sofas, away from the streets we create. Feeling good for ourselves, we're generous with other Western lives.

Generosity to other races doesn't make us kind people, because our thoughts aren't of people. There's no love in welcoming people claiming persecution without regard for the impact on people already here. There might be reason they're persecuted. They mightn't be persecuted at all.

We were compassionate, before we touted our compassion. We're no longer a compassionate community, because we're no longer compassionate or a community. Communities are compassionate to their own, but confining compassion to our own would be discriminatory. Refusing loyalties leaves us without compassion at all. We have ideology called compassion: a political expression lying not in our hearts or hands but in self-aggrandising dogma. Our crude compassion's an abstraction we cite to cut each other down.

Through the 2010 Australian election campaign, the Liberal Party promised to control Australian borders in the face of asylum seekers coming by boat. There was no reason to believe borders would be raised any more than they'd been raised in the past, but still the policy infuriated two men who confronted the party's candidate for the Hindmarsh electorate. "My poor volunteer, who was on his first day of the campaign trail, got punched in the face many times," said Jassmine Wood. "I got hit in the side of the head. My campaign volunteer was actually down on the ground with somebody sitting on his chest really hitting him in the face. The man's friend joined in, hitting my volunteer. They had an issue with the Liberal Party's stance on border protection and immigration."

Our countries have become refuges for everyone, but us. If refugee advocates felt love, care, or compassion, they wouldn't be refugee advocates. They'd be nationalists. We with our nations were kinder people than we citizens of the world have become.

14. UNSKILLED IMMIGRATION

By 2011, being homogenously British was a fault, which Hawkesbury City mayor Kim Ford was keen to refute. He expected the census data that year to reveal more Chinese immigrants, especially Asian families taking over market gardens.

Mayor Carol Provan felt the slight on the Sutherland Shire being accused of being white. She defended it by expecting the census to show a big increase in immigrants from India and China, and by boasting of being one of the most "refugee-friendly zones in Australia," with an influx of Sudanese.

When parliamentarian Craig Thomson accused the Australian government of "an appeal to the worst elements of human nature" in trying to exclude asylum seekers from the country, he wasn't just recognising our desire for national borders as being human nature. He was rejecting human nature, at least for the West.

(At the time, 2012, Thomson was subject to police investigations into the theft by him of half a million dollars from the Health Services Union when he'd been its secretary. Apparently stealing from the working-class people he was paid to represent wasn't among the worst elements of human nature.)

We presume much of what modern-day refugees might become, instead of what they are. "There are a lot of refugees who might not only be the next Albert Einstein or a good taxpayer," said Bill Shorten in September 2013 while campaigning for the leadership of the parliamentary Australian Labour Party. In fact, Einstein was already a widely renowned scientist who had been offered a position at Princeton University when he fled Nazi Germany in 1933.

Through the jobs in which I often caught taxis, I usually sat in the front seat and spoke to the drivers. Conversation normally turned to where the driver was born; only in London's black cabs did I expect drivers in Western countries to be locally born.

Slowly I realised that the strange turn of syllables with which drivers in Denmark through the 1990s replied was Iraq. They must have known their way around Baghdad better than they knew their way around Copenhagen, unless the long routes and delays while they thumbed through directories were supposed to rack up the fares.

In Sydney through those years, when driving alone, I normally listened to the radio. One interviewee discussing refugees and asylum said the Third World was full of people seizing any opportunity to enter the West.

The people we call refugees aren't looking for refuge. They're looking for money.

In 1999, the Australian government introduced temporary protection visas, which gave refugees many more rights than Asian countries gave them but no family reunion rights and no right to re-enter Australia if they departed. The visas lasted only three years, so would not be renewed if conditions improved in their homelands. The numbers of asylum seekers coming by boat plummeted.

A subsequent government replaced them with permanent protection visas in 2008. The boats returned.

In 2009, psychiatry registrar Tanveer Ahmed was surprised to discover so many people in Pakistan knew every detail of Western immigration rules. *"A taxi driver lamented the growing barriers to entering Britain,"* he wrote, *"which was once seen as a relatively easy option. A considerable number asked about gaining entry by claiming political asylum. Australia was universally seen as highly desirable but difficult to enter. New Zealand was often seen as the gateway country."* Indeed, *"there can be little doubt, the path of asylum is attractive to those without the appropriate skills or financial resources to obtain migration. It is naive to think otherwise."*

I doubt a white person could have written so candidly. From someone of another race, Ahmed's article attracted no attention, at least no comments that the *Sydney Morning Herald* newspaper published. Immigrants want better lives, with refugee status the call for people too poor and unskilled to qualify under other categories of immigration. Asylum is an excuse.

In 2011, Wise Strategic Communications, a communications company based in Kabul, advised the Australian government that Afghan Hazaras in Bamyan province weren't coming to Australia in fear of persecution, as their applications for asylum claimed, but economic deprivation. *"Lower-income classes feel their opportunities are virtually non-existent and that clandestine migration is their only option,"* said the report. "*The vast majority of focus group participants from Ghazni regard migration to Australia as a livelihood strategy and coping mechanism to respond to social and economic needs.*" The Australian government kept the report secret, until a well-crafted request under freedom of information laws led to it reaching a newspaper.

Wise conducted fifty interviews and ten focus groups among the Hazara enclaves in Afghanistan through 2010. Many Hazaras believed that reaching Australian waters practically guaranteed them refugee status. It outweighed the risks of drowning and being cheated by professional people smugglers. With patriotism unimaginable in the West, all that deterred many of them from the journey was the need to assist their country's reconstruction. Poorer, less educated Afghans felt they had little or nothing to offer Afghanistan. Less of a loss to their country, they set off for the West.

Australian Customs and Border Protection didn't procure the report to bar the Hazaras' claims for asylum but, a spokeswoman explained, because the Australian government was working with the Afghan government on a public information campaign about the dangers of people smuggling. (The West could end human trafficking in an instant by terminating the 1951 refugee convention and ending unilateral immigration, but we're not willing to do that.) When attracting other races to the West is too dangerous for them, we encourage them to stay where they are.

"The Afghans should stay in Afghanistan to build Afghanistan," said President Hamid Karzai in 2012. "There's no longer the threats that were here…those youth must come and build their own country." Almost fifteen hundred Afghan asylum seekers were in Australian immigration detention, ninety-seven of them awaiting judicial review of their refugee rejections. Australian courts had blocked the Australian government from forcing an Afghan back to Afghanistan. Only two had returned there voluntarily.

In 2015, Afghan entrepreneur Farshid Ghyasi and economist Ahmed Siar Khoreishi complained that Afghan companies were losing their best, young employees in the wave of a hundred and sixty thousand Afghans seeking asylum in Europe that year alone. Emigration damaged Afghanistan and its economy, but the relatively rich of poor countries are relatively poor in rich ones. "If they live abroad they become dishwashers," President Ashraf Ghani told German broadcaster *Deutsche Welle*. "They don't become part of the middle class."

Had those Afghans remained in Afghanistan, building the country, might the country have resisted the Taliban takeover in 2021? The West did not care. The Taliban takeover proved a chance for the West to welcome still more refugees.

Australians complain about our compatriots setting off to America and Europe in pursuit of money and opportunity. In an economic history lecture during my university studies in Commerce, I pointed out that countries from which educated immigrants come might suffer from losing their émigrés. Everyone laughed: my fellow students, the lecturer. They fobbed off the notion of any cost to the country of origin, but an Asian leader had recently complained that Australia only accepted relatively skilled and educated Asian immigrants, rather than their seething slum-dwellers.

Early in 2012, when Iranians were among the asylum seekers reaching Australia, I met an Iranian couple in the library at my eldest daughters' high school. "Are you refugees?" I asked them.

"No." She was qualified in computing (I think it was). They came as immigrants. If they'd both been unqualified, they could've been refugees.

Pastor Guy and his wife spent time helping Iranian and Afghan refugees in Parramatta, where Guy was surprised to learn several had returned on holiday to the countries in which they supposedly feared persecution. He dutifully informed his local parliamentarian. The Australian government was already aware of the practice.

The West's refugee regimes are immigration mechanisms like any other, pointed towards the same end along different means. Refugees are the lows in immigration, unless lying and fraud constitute skills. In the West, they might.

Holyman Limited operated ferries between Belgium and England in 1997. It ensured that all passengers boarding in Oostende carried passports, but those intending to claim refugee status in England threw their passports into the Channel before alighting in Ramsgate, my colleague Fred told me. Australian Department of Immigration and Citizenship figures revealed eighty percent of asylum seekers coming to Australia by boat between 2008 and '10 threw away their passports before entering Australian waters.

We don't mind. Different countries operate differently, so

without much difficulty, we find reason to designate people wanting to come or to stay refugees. Their telling us they're refugees is often enough, although bureaucrats, courts, and tribunals like a little bit more.

Prosperous, democratic South Korea wasn't an obvious source of refugees to Canada in 2006. Ji-Hye Kim based her claim for asylum on having an abusive father and threats from South Korean moneylenders. The case became a media item because Immigration and Refugee Board judge Steve Ellis allegedly told her he would deny her claim, unless she slept with him.

Refugees are fleeing any circumstance not as good as their lives could be in the generous West. Whatever benefit they're pursuing, is the disadvantage they're leaving behind.

We perceive persecution in morality no longer ours. In 2011, the Australian Refugee Review Tribunal granted asylum to a Muslim because his former wife told his family in Lebanon he was homosexual. The tribunal called him a "courageous witness," making him sound heroic, but she'd sponsored his coming from Lebanon in 2008 to marry him.

"Despite the popular view that Lebanon is the gay-friendliest country in the Arab world," the tribunal found, "some activists say that behind closed doors, sexual minorities often suffer physical and psychological abuse." (We place great credence in the testimony of homosexuals.) "Consequently, the tribunal accepts that to require the applicant to modify his behaviour in the event that he returns to Lebanon by concealing or suppressing his homosexuality, including the nature of his relationship with the witness, would amount to a persecutory curtailment of his sexual identity."

All sorts of claims of disadvantage in a country can found refugee status, even if the same disadvantage exists in the West. The Victorian police commissioner had admitted police in that state didn't prosecute domestic violence as they should, but still the Australian High Court said the same failing of the Pakistan police entitled a Pakistani woman suffering horrific domestic violence at the hands of her husband to refugee status.

Seven decades onward, the Holocaust remains at the heart of our accepting asylum seekers, no matter the cost to our countries in doing so. We accept them because we didn't accept all the Jews fleeing Nazism before World War II.

Some we did accept were Walter Bass and his family in 1939, although I saw no evidence of gratitude from him. Bass went onto become among the most prolific letter writers to the *North Shore Times* newspaper. His letter published the last Friday in January 2009 came under a heading featured in bold type across the centre of the newspaper page, which a journalist might have drafted: 'Our traditional warm welcome must return.'

Bass insisted that Afghans and Sri Lankans coming in 2009 *"were fleeing from very much the same situations I and my family had been subjected to some fifty years before."* In his view, treating asylum seekers *"with suspicion,"* which seemed to mean anything less than trusting them completely, *"cost six million lives."*

In fact, there is nothing remotely comparable between Jews fleeing the Holocaust and modern-day asylum seekers. No Jew returned to functioning Auschwitz on holiday, buying souvenirs and taking photographs, as modern-day refugees return to the countries from which we've granted them asylum. For all the failings in the world, no genocides are under way. We're not saving their lives by admitting them.

Bass went onto abuse the *"microphonic mischief-makers"* who, safely within the anonymity of talkback radio, expressed their freedom to speak of their feelings and bad experiences of *"selected minority groups."* Bass considered them morally no different to the perpetrators of the Holocaust: the Nazis. He hated those *"anonymous callers"* with the venom that in many a letter he'd laid upon the previous Australian government's *"disgraceful denigration"* of asylum seekers. (I'd never heard such hatred from those he was eager to silence.)

We applaud our relationships with countries, while granting asylum to their citizens. It's much like granting refuge to Jews fleeing the Holocaust, while lauding our relationship with the Nazis.

Early in 2012, Golden Cross Resources Limited sent the managing director Kim and a Chinese director Jingmin to an Australia China Business Council networking day in Canberra. Prime Minister Julia Gillard was one of several Australian political leaders gushing over the Chinese.

A few weeks later, ten Chinese members of the Falun Gong spiritual movement sailing their way to New Zealand to claim asylum landed in Darwin. Concerned their boat mightn't last the journey to New Zealand, the Australian government persuaded them to seek asylum in Darwin. "I obviously think that's a good outcome," said immigration minister Chris Bowen, "as it means they won't be yet again taking another further dangerous boat journey." Not simply granting refugee rights, we're persuading people to stay.

At the same time, an international property fair in Beijing offered Chinese buyers Western real estate. "*Invest in property*," boasted one sign, "*speedy migration*."

"*Buy Australian real estate*," said another sign, "*free migration*."

Western countries aren't just for sale. They're for sale at fairs. They come with immigration. Buying property in Cyprus offered a buyer the European Union.

"Will you only consider Australia for migration?" asked one investor. Immigration was a little more complicated than just buying the land.

"What about Canada?" was the reply.

Joining Falun Gong or another cult with a boat might've been easier for some than buying properties. The result would be the same.

The refugee industry is more marketing of the West's open borders to a Western populace wanting so much to be kind. Behind it lie the same sectional commercial interests wanting other immigration.

Addressing the Infrastructure Partnerships Australia conference in 2010 was Ross Rolfe, chief executive of Alinta Energy, a member of the board of Infrastructure Australia, and a former Queensland co-ordinator general. Referring to the recent federal election, he wanted "the population and boat people debate to fade into the distance."

Tony Shepherd, the chairman of Transfield Services and toll road operator Connect East Group, said the debate (such as it was) had been "terrible." As usual, he claimed Australia had benefited from immigration, but went onto laud asylum seekers above all other immigrants. "If you've got the gumption to go across in a leaky boat across the Timor Sea and arrive here, it is almost a pre-qualification." Commoditising them with his forebears, Shepherd equated them with Early Settlers who built the country. "We are all fundamentally, other than our indigenous population, and even they probably too, we are all fundamentally boat people."

Baulderstone managing director Rick Turchini equated the birth of our children with the coming of asylum seekers. "On the one hand," he said, "we are talking about restricting boat people, and on the other hand, we are paying baby bonuses."

Stockland managing director Matthew Quinn insisted an aging population demanded economic growth, while deriding Australian homes amidst the pressures of population growth. "The quarter-acre block is basically killing the Australian city because it means you have to go further and further out, and the radial transport links just get further and further from the core." He wanted more high-density housing. Stockland was a property developer.

The conference was another Western frenzy for economic expansion without considering the consequences: refugees for economic growth. "Surely we've got to continue to grow or we start to decay," said Chris Lynch, chief executive of toll road owner Transurban.

Only the West reduces the future to either economic growth or decay, but growth can't be infinite. Decay becomes inevitable.

15. THE DEATH OF DISCUSSION

For all the nice people from other races we know, we have more than enough reason to think our descendants will suffer more than we suffer from mass indiscriminate immigration. I've never met a person who'd rationally examined races and cultures to conclude open borders won't condemn us. I've only met people who refuse to consider the possibility. They frown upon, if not berate, those who do. They're the people with whom I'm trying to converse.

Among the raucous demonstrations against racism I've seen broadcast on television news programmes over decades, one particularly memorable huge banner neatly summarised the multiculturalist West. As I recall, it was suitably coloured red, for all the rage it bore down upon people who might bravely utter forth. *"Racism: Don't debate it, destroy it!"*

Debate be damned. Even when Jean-Marie Le Pen was the only other candidate left in the 2002 French presidential elections, incumbent Jacques Chirac refused to debate a racist.

Ours are conflicts without conversation. We don't fail to persuade. We refuse to discuss.

Our Western right of free speech has become the right of loud voices to drown out gentle speakers, whose right is to whisper so no one can hear. We can't stop people shouting louder than we do, even if they're so busy shouting they don't pause to speak and don't care to listen. We have no right to be heard but a right to be ignored, if we're fortunate.

We demonise dissidents, without distraction wasting time considering their words. The insult second only to being called racist is being called xenophobic: the brand scolded into the flesh of people not enthusiastically wanting more immigrants. So much as questioning the alleged economic, social, and cultural benefits of boundless immigration, wondering whether it's a good idea after all, is symptomatic of xenophobia: a supposedly irrational fear of foreigners.

Xenophobia is like bigotry and racism. It's an affliction only white people suffer.

There's no word for rationally questioning multiculturalism, wondering whether our lives would be better without other races so near. A phobia can only be irrational, making the dissident the issue. It's reminiscent of old communist dictatorships sending dissidents to psychiatric asylums. Knowing that communism was patently the perfect political and economic system, they reasoned that anyone who couldn't see that perfection must be mentally ill.

We feel the same for unending immigration. Presuming that all sane people want to do is work, spend, and watch sport, we think white people valuing their race, culture, or country are insane. Immersed in our individualism, we think something's wrong with white people caring about other white people.

The third Wednesday morning in November 2009, I sat with Pastor Guy in the David Jones store cafeteria in Hornsby. So remarkably well-informed was he about the situation in the Netherlands, I came to wonder if that might have been the land of his forebears. He believed the Dutch were abandoning their liberalism since the Second World War, but within a generation from then, only a minority of babies born in the Netherlands would be Dutch.

Two decades earlier, he'd been a New South Wales parliamentarian. Knocking on the doors of homes in Hurstville, people told him of their anxiety about Asian immigration. They must've felt he would keep their confidences, because they complained they weren't otherwise free to mention it. Theirs were the voices forbidden to speak.

"We still can't talk about it," I responded.

The futures of Western races aren't open for discussion, unless we welcome our decline. Rarely need anyone wave a court order stopping us from speaking, but judges are the least formidable of our foes. The law protects words and ideas of commercial value with copyright and patents, but abandons all others. We're glad when it doesn't prohibit them.

Late in the 1980s, I'd been living in Meadowbank. Walking from my sunlit home unit to the railway station, I saw by chance a former colleague of mine with thick, wiry blonde hair: a law firm paralegal, performing legal work without solicitor qualifications. "There are too many Asians in Meadowbank," she lamented. "I'm not a racist, my boyfriend is Indian, but I just think there are too many."

In 1984, historian Geoffrey Blainey told a group of Rotarians in Warrnambool, Victoria that most Australians didn't support the high rate of Asian immigration, provoking great protests. Fellow academics forced him to resign from the University of Melbourne four years later. We learned to keep quiet.

A decade would pass before Australia's best known dissident, a red-haired parliamentarian from Queensland, spoke up. All this time onward, I can't repeat her name without arousing passions I'm trying not to arouse. No politician since then has spoken as she spoke during her single term.

In her 1996 maiden speech, she spoke of race, but not as a matter of shame or obligation. She suggested Aborigines should receive government assistance according to their financial need and not purely for being Aboriginal. Opposing multiculturalism and the high levels of Asian immigration changing Australia, she made the incredible suggestion, in the West, of controlling immigration, paying regard to public opinion within a country (instead of merely outside it). "Of course," she said, "I will be called racist but, if I can invite whom I want into my home, then I should have the right to have a say in who comes into my country."

Amidst the resulting furore, public figures treated her like a fool. Being the member for Oxley, she was the "Oxley moron."

A brief newspaper profile of actor John Waters included the words he'd say to her if he met her: in a very, very slow-speaking voice as he would address an imbecile, "One fish and chips, please." That she operated a paltry fish and chips shop before entering parliament was more reason to dismiss her.

Commentators claimed her comments harmed Australia's reputation in Asia, although Asian countries didn't allow the immigration Australia did. Worst of all, at least one commentator claimed her comments harmed Australia's business interests, although an Australian ambassador to Indonesia told a seminar I attended all that mattered was how keen parties were to do business anyway.

A mother of four children, she copped more abuse when, caring for her country, she said she felt like the mother of Australia. The Sydney Mardi Gras parade included several homosexual men prancing about in misogynistic mockery of her, dressed in loud red wigs, thick make-up, and bright dresses. We tormented her for not welcoming the end of our country, for liking what the country had been.

She and her supporters were damned, derided, and denigrated, but were rarely, if ever, debated. Anyone not quick to despise her was lumbered with the title redneck, as we call white racists. (Only white people can have red necks.) Australian musical group Midnight Oil (whose lead singer Peter Garrett identified as a Christian and would later enter federal parliament too, becoming a cabinet minister) recorded the derisory album *Redneck Wonderland*, with the song 'White Skin Black Heart.' Pauline Hanson (there, I said it) suffered the most vicious, relentless abuse I'd seen waged upon anyone.

The cruellest parody of all came from Simon, who had been a school friend of mine. I'd not seen Simon since school when I first saw him in a newspaper, completely bald, convening a festival of homosexual and other queer cinema. I was then unaware that he had propositioned a boy at a party near the end of our schooling.

Simon next appeared in a newspaper calling himself Pauline Pantsdown, donning a dress, red wig, and make-up to mock Pauline Hanson. As good satire does, the impersonations accentuated her features, but with a grotesque hardness to her lips, face, and frown, as homosexual men often see in women. They spoke more of Simon's perceptions of her (and how he wanted others to perceive her) than anything real about her.

He released a song synthesising and parodying her voice into the most twisted and squeaky of lower-class accents, as the product of a prestigious private school can. His song was no reasoned engagement but very funny, cleverly constructed cruelty, editing words from her speeches so she was calling herself a man, prostitute, and agent for the Ku Klux Klan. The song so personally targeted made her weep, but the government-owned JJJ radio network played it relentlessly for a week before being served with a court injunction to cease. The song was defamatory for calling her a transsexual prostitute.

Several times in costume and with journalists eager to witness, Simon sought to confront her. She eluded him.

He produced a second song, repeating a handful of her words over and over to make her sound like an idiot. JJJ repeatedly played that song too, particularly through the next federal election campaign. With the major parties directing their preferences against her and with a gaffe on taxation policy, she lost her parliamentary seat.

At our twenty-year school reunion, I asked Simon about his Hanson songs. He smiled. "It made her cry," I told him, of the first song at least.

"She upset Aboriginal people."

I wondered what Aboriginal people Simon knew. He hated white racism so much.

My Hong Kong Chinese friend Ted, also at the reunion, championed tolerance and diversity for the West, but not tolerance towards white people wanting to keep our countries or diversity of opinion about it. He told me he applauded Simon for the song, although not because of Hanson's comments about Aborigines. "She's made a lot of Asian people feel unwelcome," he said. Ted then relayed to me the story of an Asian man in a queue who'd been told by a white Australian that he would soon have to leave the country for what Hanson was doing.

"He shouldn't have done that," I told Ted, but that didn't excuse the songs Simon sang. "No one should make a song just to make a person cry. She's a human being."

Ted remained unmoved. He was loyal to his race. Hanson was loyal to ours. Simon wasn't.

What's happening in the West isn't simply with our ignorance, but with our conviction in the truth of matters untrue. Amidst the abuse Australians meted out upon Hanson the second Sunday in November 2010, after she'd come back from Britain because of the immigrants there, was a news website reader commenting that the only countries without immigrants were those like secretive despotic North Korea. It was untrue.

We presume immigration is the norm. It isn't, but we're not wondering why other races hang onto their birthrights. We're not even noticing.

Almost a decade had passed after Hanson's maiden speech to parliament before someone dared dissent so publicly again. In a letter to his local newspaper in 2005, Andrew Fraser, an associate professor in public law at Macquarie University, linked Sudanese refugees with crime. A Sudanese complained to the Human Rights and Equal Opportunity Commission, which compelled Fraser to apologise for any offence his remarks caused.

Fraser also said interracial immigration meant Australia risked becoming a Third World colony. He wanted Australia to withdraw from the 1951 refugee convention because of the people it admitted. (He could also have referred to political and legal interpretations of the convention, although conventions are easier to leave than governments and courts are easily persuaded.) At a university where one third of students were foreign citizens on student visas (attractive to universities because they paid greater fees than Australians paid), Fraser complained that Australians were missing out on university admissions.

He went onto say Australia was allowing an Asian ruling class to develop, presumably contemplating something like Chinese economic power in Indonesia and Malaysia. Fraser's mistake was to complain about it. Complaining about powerful people is racist, whenever they're not white.

None of those remarks would have been controversial in countries defending their own. Having reached university, white people don't care about other white people who haven't. Empathising with our race is racist.

Empathising with other races is not. A newspaper columnist wrote passionately of the offence Africans felt in response to Fraser's remarks about Sudanese, wanting readers to soothe those vulnerable Africans. Their feelings were more important than those of the professor or any victims of crime.

The Macquarie University vice chancellor called Fraser's remarks repugnant. She rebuked him for speaking out of his area of expertise, although the matter was more his expertise than hers. The university pressed him to retire. He refused. He'd been lecturing for twenty-nine years, but the university's director of human resources suspended him from teaching, claiming threats from the professor's supporters would prevent his critics from exercising their rights to disagree with him. (There seem not to have been any such threats, but that didn't matter.)

Fraser wrote that the vice chancellor had "*sacrificed the time-honoured traditions of academic freedom to the illegitimate demands of ethnic pressure groups and political extremists determined to impose an ideological dictatorship upon Australian universities.... Universities once prided themselves on their commitment to the search for truth; to suppress data well-known to psychologists, criminologists, historians and legal academics merely because the truth might cause 'hurt and distress' to certain protected minorities calls into question the whole point and purpose of the University.*"

Formerly centrepieces of intellectual debate, academic bodies had become centrepieces in stifling debate. *"For those who are disturbed by his comments,"* decreed the university student council, *"please ignore it because this man is just: FULL OF S**T!"*

I don't know exactly what about Fraser's comments meant he was so full of it. The council didn't need to explain.

We're so proud of our libertarian visions we can't see our new totalitarianism: the tyranny of individualism. Australians complain about asylum seekers coming by boat, expressing concern for their well-being and other refugees whose places they take, because we're not allowed to talk about immigration. Were other races on earth under siege but forbidden from mentioning it, they'd enter the West claiming asylum. We have nowhere to go.

In 2015, faculty member Erika Christakis complained about a Yale University memorandum telling faculty and students not to wear Halloween costumes that could offend students from minority races. *"American universities were once a safe space not only for maturation but also for a certain regressive, or even transgressive, experience,"* she wrote, *"increasingly, it seems, they have become places of censure and prohibition."*

Amidst an encounter between Christakis' husband (another faculty member) and hostile protesters demanding both their resignations, one coloured protester yelled at him: *"It is not about creating an intellectual space! It is not! Do you understand that? It is about creating a home here!"*

The West is no longer home for white people. Macquarie University, which punished Andrew Fraser for espousing truth, was the same university where, a dozen years earlier, I'd studied philosophy.

16. NATIONALITY WITHOUT NATIONALISM

"Patriotism is the last refuge of a scoundrel," said Englishman Samuel Johnson in 1775. Today, we quote Johnson's words to criticise patriotism, but he intended them to criticise scoundrels, knowing how generous of heart patriots are.

Reversing the words from American John Kennedy's presidential inauguration address in 1961, Western peoples ask not what we can do for our countries but what our countries can do for us. People with no sense of nation still want their countries to bail them out of trouble into which they've dumped themselves.

Single-person citizenship is ours to pick or reject. Nations without nationalism don't remain nations for long.

"Two thousand years ago, the proudest boast was *civis romanus sum*," said Kennedy in 1963. I am a citizen of Rome. By 1963, the proudest boast was *"Ich bin ein Berliner."* I am a Berliner.

By the 1980s, the boast of the West was, "I've got access to money." Needing the permits to live, work, and travel that come with citizenship somewhere, people buy nationality in the West like buying horseradish. Hong Kong businessmen wanting to immigrate to Australia just needed enough money in their bank accounts, until the Australian government realised that funds were transferred into those accounts before they applied. After the applications were accepted, the funds were returned to their owners or transferred to other applicants' accounts.

Western governments aren't the only governments to sell citizenship. White people are the only people not to care.

The Kingdom of Tonga never lost its sovereignty to European empires but in 1983, the Tongan government began offering passports for purchase by Hong Kong Chinese fearing Beijing's rule after 1997. When Tongans discovered the illegal sales of a mere four hundred passports in 1991, they demanded the government cancel the citizenship of citizens they'd never seen anyway.

Chinese could live in Tonga with work permits. By 2006, they'd become obvious among the shops in the capital Nuku' alofa. Notwithstanding that the Chinese numbered only three or four percent of the population and many more Tongans had emigrated to other countries, rioters looting and burning government buildings demanding democracy also attacked more than thirty Chinese-operated stores.

The riots succeeded. The Tongan government didn't renew the Chinese work permits. Several hundred Chinese emigrated.

Western citizenship isn't a privilege. It's a product for sale. In 2013, Malta's parliament approved selling Maltese citizenship for six hundred and fifty thousand euros, entitling purchasers to carry Maltese passports, live in the European Union, and travel visa-free to America.

The Australian government advertises citizenship to permanent residents, much as hawkers tout sideshows at a fair. (Governments can't help themselves from advertising something.) Immigration to America has been offered in banner advertisements on computer sites.

Immigration to Canada was offered by electronic mail to everyone in the Harry Chapin group at *Yahoo!* the second Saturday in October 2010, with the message, "*Discover How You Can Immigrate to Canada Click here....*" I wouldn't have minded so much if the invitation was personal, but it was the ubiquitous spam used to sell pornography, sex aids, and mail order brides.

Residency is a game to be won, entirely by chance. Every year since 1995, the American government has offered fifty-five thousand (fifty thousand from 1999) green card residency permits by worldwide lottery, exempting only those countries from which fifty thousand immigrants have come through the preceding five years.

More publicly than the United Kingdom, America made racial diversity a stated ambition of her immigration programme. She preferred a multitude of races coming through her borders to the bad old days when almost all immigrants were European.

America might have feared a single race prevailing. The New Zealander company secretary at Otter Gold Mines Limited thought Australia fared better with our polyglot of races than New Zealand with a single dominant racial minority. At the time, 2000, I didn't think to press Peter about his experience. New Zealand's Maoris was obviously causing problems I'd never read in the news.

A practical notion in 1868 when immigrants were Europeans who'd come there by boat, the Fourteenth Amendment to the American Constitution conferred rights of citizenship on people born in the country. A century and a half later, children of illegal immigrants argue they're akin to descendants of the first colonials born on American soil. They're the anchor babies, trying to secure child and family in America.

It facilitates birthing tourism. Hidden in American suburbs are maternity centres, where Chinese women prepare before giving birth in American hospitals and rest afterwards, advertised in wealthy Chinese cities.

Dwight Chang of Arcadia, California operated such a centre on residential Palm Avenue, San Gabriel until 2011, when it was shut down for breaching building codes. "There was a constant barrage of pregnant women going in and out of the house," observed Taylor Anderson, of the three identical two-storey townhouses that appeared from the outside like any other Spanish-style homes with red-tiled roofs.

"If they lived here, I don't mind," said Duke Trinh, whose home was nearby. "If they are running a business, I don't want them here. It's not fair for us if" the mothers "go back to China and later send their kids here for" free public "education, because they don't pay taxes, we do."

Nationality means more outside the West, where countries reserve citizenship to their own. They equate nation and race, much as the West does rejecting both. Their countries continue.

In the Western world, nationality no longer equates to a race. We freely grant citizenship to people who want it, for as long as they do. We created nation states but now reduce them to paper-thin citizenship, which can change by the stroke of a bureaucratic key. When a new offer outshines the old, we can change Western nationalities as readily as our forebears changed boxer short underpants, if it suits us to do so.

With Western countries trivialising our citizenships, there's little wonder the rest of the world trivialises ours too. I can't recall how many passports my fellow business student James possessed in his life. Four, I think, including Malaysia where he was born and Britain. Nor can I recall how many were still current when last he sat in our home. Two, I think, namely Australia and New Zealand.

At the time he was visiting Sydney while working in the land of his ancestors: China.

Popular lore says the easiest means to Australian citizenship is taking New Zealand citizenship for however many years. Australia's fraternal relationship with New Zealand extends to people who've just arrived. Fraternity has become fairly brief in the West.

Without race, we're simply citizens, but passing nationalities mean nothing. People fleeting into my country don't become my compatriots because of the forms they file and fees they pay, nor even the taxes we imagine they'll remunerate. We're not suddenly bonded and then suddenly not when they fleet out again. If we were, then our bonding is too brittle to mean anything to either of us.

Western citizenships being transient, identities based upon them are equally transient. Western countries allowing dual citizenship mean that if nationality were identity, those dual citizens would be schizophrenic, or simply two-faced. Claiming identity with one face and not the other would be no less schizophrenic.

Australian citizenship had become so meaningless that in 2011, Southport District Court recognised New Zealand sailor Bill Goodhue as a de facto Australian citizen because he'd visited the country often enough. "I know a lot of New Zealanders," said Judge Clive Wall, "and they would describe themselves as residents of both countries." They "come and go on a regular basis."

We let people flow freely across borders. We don't discriminate between good people and bad.

In 2010, the Administrative Appeals Tribunal allowed a convicted sex offender known as D.N.C.W. to remain in Australia after his release from prison for raping his girlfriend and attempting to rape his stepdaughter because he was "virtually an Australian person," in the words of the tribunal's senior member, John Handley. "He supports an Australian Rules football team. He also enjoys tennis, volleyball, badminton, and soccer. He enjoys motorbike and motor car racing and his hero was Peter Brock." Returning him to Malta would've thus caused him "hardship" and been "unfair" (although Brock being dead meant the rapist was no more likely to see him in Melbourne than Malta).

Western countries become patches and portions of earth, to which anyone can come and remain. Our identities become bits and pieces of land: a street, suburb, or city. We're Londoners for living there, before becoming Los Angelinos because we've changed address. We cease being what we were and become something else by changing abode. Changing identity so readily is superficial and shallow, among people passing through or staying a while. We might be comfortable, even happy, but we belong in one place no more than we belonged in the last. We have nowhere we belong, just places we reside.

Of all the identities to choose in our post-racial West, none are more transient. If nationality is a weak identity for being merely a legal descriptor, then geographical identity doesn't even require a legal right to reside. If accidents of geography are all we have to call ourselves a country, then it's not very much.

We've become itinerant, but we're not nomads by nature. Even the Bedouin recognise their link to the deserts around which they wander.

Growing up in Sydney when Australia was still a country, I often visited suburban Ashfield. Marking the corner my father or mother turned the car towards my maternal great-aunts' homes was the Arnott's biscuit factory, with its distinctive cream-coloured clock tower keeping time. The car windows didn't need to be open for us to smell the hot biscuits baking. Away from Parramatta Road, the softly elegant brown-brick houses with white-painted windowpanes harked from Australia's Federation era, around 1901.

My mother's family was once prominent in Ashfield, providing my great-aunts with great wealth. The last surviving sibling was my Great-Aunt Dulcie, a childless widow. More than her extended family, her devotion in the 1970s was to Vietnamese refugees.

Dulcie died unmourned in 1995. No Vietnamese came to her funeral.

What her forebears called their family wealth, their race's wealth, Dulcie had decided was hers alone. Her last will and testament reflected her sense of being the righteous individual, without recognition of how much she owed her family. The woman who had inherited enough money never to work could have bequeathed it to her niece (my aunt) to make her life easier, but didn't. Doubtlessly she felt good for giving away family money to charities when she couldn't use it anymore.

We're doing the same with our countries. We give our inheritances to strangers, as if they were only ours to give.

In 2007, I made a rare return to Ashfield. What most had changed were the people, but people are everything. They always were. Ashfield had become Chinese.

Back in 2004, Macquarie University researcher Amanda Wise had found older residents resented the lack of signs in English along the Ashfield main street, lack of design quality, and the predominance of Chinese-language menus displayed in restaurant windows. Ashfield Council and local business groups began a Building Neighbourhood Community Harmony programme in 2006, so most shops carried parallel English and Mandarin signage.

In 2011, the *Sydney Morning Herald* newspaper spoke of 'Old Ashfield now new Shanghai: The inner west suburb is a microcosm of Sydney's new face.' Researcher Duanfang Lu, from the Faculty of Architecture, Design, and Planning at the University of Sydney, said Ashfield demonstrated that immigration changes not just an area's demographics but its physical environment. "While its main commercial streets had a mix of Anglo, Italian, and Greek shopping before the mid 1990s, about eighty-five percent of the shops are now Chinese small businesses, including restaurants, supermarkets, barbershops, and bookstores."

Multiculturalism had been merely a phase along the way from Ashfield being British to what Lu and others called Little Shanghai. The Crocodile Farm Hotel, previously the type of pub found in far north Queensland, had been remodelled with an Emerald Room and gaming lounge like a Macau casino. The Ashfield Presbyterian and Baptist churches hosted services in Mandarin and Cantonese. The old Goodlet Sunday School and Institute was an English language centre. The Bread of Life Christian Church of Taipei dominated a street corner.

Thomas Jin, who'd arrived thirty years earlier from Shanghai and eventually became the new mandarin of Ashfield, theorised as to why Ashfield's transformation had been so complete. "Chinese people love a Chinatown," he said. "They like to be in an environment that is familiar." Only white people don't.

Outside Ashfield railway station stood a statue of Mei Quong Tart, who'd died in 1903 unknown to Australians. There were no statues of the once pre-eminent British, such as my maternal grandfather's family, nor even my Great-Uncle Geoffrey gassed in the Great War.

Chinese history was replacing Australian history. Places no

longer ours become other people's places, as if they always were.

17. THE END OF COUNTRY

Initially, human rights were predicated upon nations and borders. Article 13 (2) of the Universal Declaration of Human Rights, 1948, grants people the right to leave countries without contemplating rights to enter them. Article 31 of the United Nations Convention Relating to the Status of Refugees, 1951, refers to "*illegal entry or presence*" in a country when saying it shouldn't disadvantage refugees.

Colonial Europeans no longer define our countries by our mother countries or European composites. In our rejection of race, it's become fashionable to redefine ours as countries of raceless people called immigrants. Some of my fellow Australians trace their families in this country longer than I can. Others supposedly Australian arrived here this morning.

We thus remove our connection to the land, making us less than our indigenous peoples. We also trivialise our forebears, sharing their credit with recent arrivals from all manner of countries, although they retain one key distinction. Recent arrivals, from outside the West, we don't call invaders.

Europe is becoming the same. Chancellor Angela Merkel described Germany in 2015 as a "country of immigration."

If ever there were an immigrant country, it would be Singapore. Singaporeans haven't redefined their country to be one of immigrants.

Redefining our countries as countries of immigrants is more than just redefinition without race. It's abandoning all notion of being countries at all. The very fact that someone comes (by whatever means and for whatever reason) makes that person a compatriot. People wanting to come aspire to be our compatriots, so we should let them come too.

Official figures in 2010 found the one-fifth of people in Switzerland who were foreigners were disproportionately more likely to be charged with crimes. A small majority of Swiss voters approved a referendum in November 2011 to deport automatically foreigners convicted of serious crimes such as murder, rape, or trafficking in drugs or people, but nothing kept human rights groups and legal experts from our uniquely Western conviction there should be no compulsion or constraints on the movements of people (at least into or out of the West). Nothing makes us revert.

"Deportation is an old idea," claimed Australian Trenton Oldfield in Britain in 2013. "It's from another time. It's from a thousand years ago."

In fact, deportation is still the norm outside the West. It was in the West until recently. In spite of the Home Office considering Oldfield's presence in Britain "undesirable," a British court excused him from deportation after he said he wasn't willing to subject his Indian wife to racist Australia.

In India that day, Naresh Rawel was also complaining about the treatment of Indians in Australia, calling his son Puneet Puneet "a victim" of supposedly racist Australia. Five years earlier, Puneet had been speeding along City Road, Melbourne with more than three times the legal limit of alcohol in his blood when he struck Gold Coast students Dean Hofstee and Clancy Coker, killing Hofstee and seriously injuring Coker.

Deportation from the West might be an old idea. Fleeing our jurisdiction isn't. Before being sentenced for culpable driving, Puneet fled Australia on a friend's passport. He later worked in an Indian call centre.

We evict foreign citizens convicted of crimes, but it's selective eviction. We deport them to other Western countries, as Australia did returning convicted paedophile Raymond Horne to Britain in 2008.

With other races, we're more tolerant. The Australian government wanted to deport Patricia Toia, a "one-woman crime wave" with her many criminal convictions including heroin trafficking, back to New Zealand in 2007, but the land of her birth didn't want her.

An Australian refugee action collective wanted her. Australia should "help Ms Toia with her problems, not deport her," said a spokesman. Refugees were everyone wanting to live here: everyone for us to help.

Instead of criminals, we have people with problems. Immigration means importing other country's problems, making them ours.

We don't deport criminals to countries imposing punishments to which we object. Chinese double-murderer Wang Zhen remained in an Australian detention centre after completing his fifteen-year-sentence in an Australian gaol, because we were concerned China might execute him for his crimes.

Accused of kidnapping and murder in China in 1996, Interpol wanted a Chinese citizen arrested in March 2004. He then spent eight years in detention in Australia, participating in almost thirty cases of *"disturbances, abusive/aggressive behaviour, assault, voluntary starvation, self-harm, and having a prohibited article."* Nevertheless, Australia granted him a bridging visa in 2012, because Chinese authorities might torture him and impose the death penalty upon him.

If that wasn't enough, the Human Rights and Equal Opportunity Commission awarded him fifteen thousand dollars compensation for being moved between two detention centres in a one-person compartment in a ten-seat Mercedes. It violated *"the dignity, privacy, and care needs of individual detainees."*

Released and free to work in Australia without telling prospective employers about the accusations against him, his rights prevailed over any rights we had even to know his name. Australia's human rights obligations apparently demanded it, as they don't demand protection for Australians.

We're not just the world's policemen. We're the world's correctional services. The logical corollary to the accommodations we grant criminals is inviting the rest of the world to send us its criminals who face execution, lashings, or other punishments we consider too harsh, if that's what they want. We can gaol them in the West, or impose whatever lesser punishments (like sitting in the corner of the room for an hour or so) we consider appropriate.

Illegally entering countries outside the West is normally a crime. Illegally entering Western countries normally isn't. (Not every illegal act is a crime.)

The first day of July 2011, President Barack Obama opposed an Arizona law making illegal immigration into America a crime. Immigration wasn't among the laws he imagined when he said that "no matter how decent" the eleven million illegal immigrants in America were, they should be held accountable for breaking the law.

In the West's gluttony for globalism came the catchphrase, "No one is ever illegal." The second day of April 2013, Associated Press (which called itself the world's most trusted news organisation) executive editor Kathleen Carroll explained that only an action and not a person could be illegal. Illegal immigration doesn't make people illegal immigrants, not in the West.

It's like saying no one is ever a criminal. Some people simply commit crimes. (By 2016, America's Department of Justice was referring to criminals as "justice-involved individuals.")

People who would be illegal immigrants elsewhere (thrashed with a cane and deported from Singapore) had become undocumented immigrants in the West. They happened to have come or stayed without completing proper procedures. At least since 2012 in America, they've been undocumented Americans, although Associated Press media relations director Paul Colford rejected the term "undocumented" immigrants for being imprecise. Instead, they were people "living in" or "entering a country illegally" or "without legal permission." People brought into the country as children weren't to be described as entering the country illegally.

The previous evening, April Fools' Day 2013, Jose Zarate had asked Maria Saucedo in Aguila, Arizona if he could pursue a romantic relationship with her thirteen-year-old daughter. She refused, so in front of her daughter, he shot her dead. The *Phoenix Times* newspaper didn't mention his immigration status. *Fox* television news did. "Sheriff's deputies say Zarate is a non-US citizen who has been living in the country without proper authorisation."

We've reduced Western countries to matters of paperwork. Western borders are coming down altogether.

Trivialising illegal immigration to mere irregularity, Australia had begun calling illegal immigrants coming by boat "irregular maritime arrivals" after a change in government in 2007. We don't punish them. We help them. Immigration department and detention centre staff began calling them "clients."

The Australian Press Council guideline 288 of 2009 said describing people as *"illegal immigrants"* or *"illegals?"* could breach its Standards of Practice. It preferred *"over-stayers"* or *"asylum seekers."*

When another change in government restored reference to immigrants being illegal in 2013, Labour Party immigration

SIMON LENNON

spokesman Richard Marles objected. "It's really important that Australia treats every human being with respect."

Those human beings needn't respect us or our borders. We don't.

By May 2014, the *Australian Broadcasting Corporation News* had dispensed with adjectives altogether, referring simply to migrants. Up to seventy of them from Somalia, Syria, and Eritrea illegally entering Europe from Turkey had been aboard a boat that capsized in the Aegean Sea. Greek authorities had so far rescued thirty-six and taken them to Athens.

Corrupting our convictions of universal rights to discriminate in favour of ourselves would be incomprehensible, but we discriminate in favour of others. Santa Ana College, a public community college in California, set up a scholarship in 2010 not simply open to immigrants, including those in America illegally, but restricted to them. The rationale was a drunk driver in May killing illegal immigrant Tan Ngoc Tran.

Her illegality hadn't harmed her studies for a doctorate degree at Brown University, where Rancho Santiago Community College District spokesman Laurie Weidner called Tran "a wonderful student leader." She'd been part of what they called the Dream Team (which didn't mean she'd been sleeping). She'd been campaigning for passage of the Dream Act: a bill to accommodate illegal immigrants further, giving them the same benefits America gives Americans (including access to scholarship money). Tran came from a country that punished and expelled illegal immigrants, so America must've seemed like a dream.

In 2011, the Maryland House of Delegates passed a law allowing illegal immigrants the same rights as other residents to discounted tuition rates at the state's community colleges. When they finished those courses, they had the same rights at the state's four-year higher education institutions.

In 2013, Colorado became the latest American state where taxpayers funded the discounting of tuition fees for the children of illegal immigrants. "*Undocumented kids will now have a fair and equitable way to pursue a higher education in CO,*" wrote Governor John Hickenlooper. We think nothing's fairer and more equitable than giving money to people whose parents violated our national borders. "*Well done.*"

Rights have consequences, but we're unconcerned about

consequences. We just care about rights.

In 2014, Guatemalan mother Nora Griselda Bercian Diaz told a Texas television station that the word in her country was "go to America with your child, you won't be turned away." So she did, enduring harassment in Tampico, escaping an attempt by members of the Zetas drug cartel to kidnap them, and bribing Mexican federal police and immigration officers. Far from fearing American Border Patrol agents, she looked for them.

The converse to Tran's death was the eight cyclists killed later in 2010 when a speeding car crashed into them in Lamezia Terme, Italy. Tucked near the end of the short news report was mention the driver was a Moroccan man who'd been smoking marihuana.

A few months earlier, illegal immigrant Carlos Martinelly Montano was awaiting deportation when he drove while intoxicated in Virginia. It would be his third charge for driving while intoxicated in five years, his licence already having been revoked. This time, his car collided with a car carrying three Catholic Benedictine nuns from Richmond. Sisters Charlotte Lange and Connie Lupton were flown to hospital in critical condition. Sister Denise Mosier died at the scene.

Homeland Security secretary Janet Napolitano promised her office would thoroughly investigate the case and make its report public, but then kept the thirty-five page report secret. Judicial Watch, a public disclosure group, obtained a copy of it through a Freedom of Information Act request. Whoever's homeland the Department of Homeland Security sought to protect, it wasn't that of three nuns in Virginia.

The report revealed federal policy quietly reducing the number of crimes that warranted deporting illegal immigrants. Northern Virginia courts and police didn't uniformly enforce laws or report their outcomes to federal immigration officials. Not only was the Immigration and Customs Enforcement agency "releasing dangerous criminal illegal aliens instead of deporting them," said Corey Stewart, chairman of the county Board of Supervisors, they issued Montano "a federal employment authorisation permit."

In 1994, Californian voters passed Proposition 187, declaring *"they have suffered and are suffering economic hardship caused by the presence of illegal immigrants in this state. That they have suffered and are suffering personal injury and damage caused by the criminal conduct of illegal immigrants in this state. That they have a right to the protection of their government from any person or persons entering this country unlawfully.*" The law restricted illegal immigrants' access to government services, but a federal judge promptly prevented it taking effect.

American courts prohibit states enforcing immigration laws for infringing upon a federal matter. They don't mind states undermining immigration laws.

In October 2013, Governor Jerry Brown recognised the impact illegal immigration was having on California. It delighted him. "California is a place of dreams," he said, making the dreams of illegal immigrants his own. "It's also a place of realities. This reality isn't about politics. It's about the people who by their fervour, their faith and their numbers transformed California." The state was becoming the tenth in America to issue driver licences to illegal immigrants.

That same day, the United Nations special rapporteur on the human rights of migrants blamed European governments because a fire had erupted on a crowded boat carrying illegal immigrants from Libya to Italy. Francois Crepeau blamed those governments not for the rewards they offered enticing immigrants to sail, but for enforcing Europe's borders at all. "Treating irregular migrants only by repressive measures would create these tragedies," he told reporters. "Irregular immigration is not a crime against persons or property or security…"

Never are the gall of other races and weakness of ours more evident than in matters of immigration. The first Saturday in October 2013, illegal immigrants and their supporters with no respect for America's borders demanded America respect them. Thousands rallied at more than forty venues across the country, in what they called a "National Day of Immigrant Dignity and Respect."

People don't need to earn respect from white people as they do from other races. They demand it, whatever they've done.

It doesn't stop. Also that day, Jerry Brown signed a raft of laws equating legal with illegal immigration. One prohibited law enforcement officials from detaining immigrants based on federal government instructions (except in cases of serious crimes or convictions). Another allowed illegal immigrants to practice law in California. A third law made it illegal for employers to discriminate between workers by their citizenship.

Liberty for immigrants leaves less liberty for the West.

California prohibited her residents from differentiating between legal and illegal immigration.

Nothing does more to spur illegal immigration than amnesty for illegal immigrants being in the wind. The Department of Homeland Security responded to massive increases in illegal immigration in 2014 not by expelling intruders, but by clothing them. It bought forty-two thousand pairs of extra-large underwear, because so many were fat.

While a candidate in 2015 for the Republican Party nomination for president, American businessman Donald Trump said that America was the "dumping ground" for the lowliest of Mexicans. Amidst the furore Trump's remarks caused, including criticisms from Mexico, commentator Ruben Navarrette described a meeting he'd attended twelve years earlier, in which a Mexican state governor said essentially the same thing.

Navarrette believed rich Mexicans privately considered their compatriots who went to America to be *"the undesirables who were out of options, didn't make it, and couldn't hack it."* Without the twenty-five billion dollars those nannies, gardeners, and others remitted home each year, he believed Mexico would be insolvent. *"Mexico gets the better end of the immigration deal since millions of people who probably couldn't be absorbed by a fragile Mexican economy instead work in the United States…"* Emigration redistributes wealth back to countries of origin.

We accommodate everyone. The trouble with no person being illegal is that no other person can ever be legal. A country without borders isn't a country; open borders aren't borders. We bring upon ourselves the end of our countries: national nothingness. Homes for everyone are homes for no one. We don't have countries anymore, but neither does anyone else, not yet.

18. THE END OF LIBERALISM

More than a million white Americans killed or wounded each other in the American Civil War, which President Abraham Lincoln justified to hold together the united states of America. (Thomas Jefferson's Declaration of Independence didn't write of united states with capital letters.) Without the Union, said Lincoln, the Declaration of Independence was just words.

Without a country to give effect to our values, they're just words. They endure only until the last paper on which they're written rots away, the last stone tablet crumbles.

Well known is Lincoln's condemnation of slavery, central to America stumbling into civil war. Unknown even to America's first black president Barack Obama was that Lincoln's Emancipation Proclamation issued in 1862 only abolished slavery in the ten Southern states that had succeeded from the Union. It was a war measure, which didn't apply to half a million slaves in states that remained with the Union: Missouri, Kentucky, Maryland, and Delaware. Lincoln didn't risk them joining the Confederacy.

"My paramount object in this struggle is to save the Union," wrote Lincoln to Horace Greeley, editor of the *New-York Tribune* newspaper, on the twenty-second day of August 1862, *"and is not either to save or to destroy slavery. If I could save the Union without freeing any slave I would do it, and if I could save it by freeing all the slaves I would do it; and if I could save it by freeing some and leaving others alone I would also do that. What I do about slavery, and the colored race, I do because I believe it helps to save the Union... I have here stated my purpose according to my view of official duty; and I intend no modification of my oft-expressed personal wish that all men everywhere could be free."*

Lincoln wasn't willing to sacrifice America in his opposition to slavery, but we're willing to sacrifice the West in our resolute opposition to racism and religious discrimination. Multicultural liberalism is our new Western ideal to which we hold fast, but changing demography means it will vote itself out of existence.

We refuse to link individual likes and beliefs to races or

religions; that would be racism or religious discrimination. We're not proud of our democracy, justice, and respect for human rights, let alone of taking them to the world, because we insist they're not ours. We think our values are universal, because we think people are. Ours are the rights we don't demand be inalienable. We think they already are.

They're not. They're more Western thought. We created liberalism. Western liberalism became Western individualism when we lost our collective senses: race, collective religion, and nation. The very presumption of values being universal is a peculiarly Western presumption.

The freedoms on which we predicate our lives are neither universal nor inalienable. They're too precious for that. We have human capacities, like thinking and speaking, but not even they're universal or inalienable.

We assume immigrants from other races will become like us because past European immigrants did, but past European immigrants were already like us. Our presumption that other races want the rights we want underlies much of our immigration and foreign policies since World War II. We're not imposing liberalism. We're releasing it.

Chris Patten, the last British governor of Hong Kong, introduced several democratic reforms soon after taking office in 1992. The reforms irritated the Chinese government, which was due to take control of the colony five years later. "Hong Kong people don't want democracy," an expatriate British lawyer told me, during a conversation on a boat trip through Hong Kong Harbour. "They just want to make money." (He was a little embarrassed to admit he enjoyed the Asian world of deferential housemaids and servants at call.)

Our desires for democracy and passions for personal freedoms aren't shared by most of the world. We see immigration in terms of individual rights afforded people who aren't individualistic.

Immigrants don't come to copy our values. They come because of them. They might come to be richer (or for their children to be richer) through jobs, government welfare payments, or medical and other resources. They might come for beaches, weather (although it's hard to imagine them headed to Scandinavia for the snow), and other aspects of our lifestyles, but not to maintain our lifestyles for us and our children.

There's no reason in reality why people pursuing admission into the West, or release from detention centres and gaols, should adopt Western values because we think they already hold them. There's even less reason their children should. Western freedoms give them rights not to do so. Multiculturalism hopes they don't.

Powerful white people imagine their comfortable lives continuing unchanged within their property walls, while they proudly maintain open borders to their countries. That swelling underclass of servants and beggars eventually become too numerous for democracy to deny them the equality those same powerful white people had offered them.

If we want to imagine our countries when we're no longer majorities, we have Venezuela to consider. The Europeans who built the country no longer dominate, amounting to only about a fifth of the population. Without nationalism, the result is socialism.

President Franklin Roosevelt's close aide Harry Hopkins argued tax and tax, spend and spend, elect and elect in America in the 1930s. He espoused a process leading to democracies that empower the fifty-one percent to elect governments taking money from the forty-nine percent.

However admirable the theory of universal suffrage, in multiracial practice, it becomes manifestly unfair. A majority race or compilation of races can democratically vote to strip wealth from minorities. It can do so from minorities rich and poor. "Democracy is two wolves and a lamb deciding what to eat for dinner," says an adage wrongly attributed to American founding father Benjamin Franklin, but an adage nevertheless. "Liberty is the lamb well-armed."

We've long qualified democracy's majority by demanding respect for minorities, before Western democracies went further and deferred to minorities. Other majorities don't.

That we no longer forge our countries in our image, not even in Europe, is no reason for other races not to forge them in theirs. Democratic rights that we espouse so passionately entitle them to choose the systems by which they live. Our ideologies of choice won't begrudge new majorities the right to impose their thinking and ways. Denying them the rights to make changes they believe to be right would be undemocratic. Demographic democracy entitles them to live by their values, demanding we do so too if they wish.

We simply can't assume we'll be free to live by our values as we become smaller parts of our national populations. Minority races not getting in our way do so when they're big enough. Substantial enough minorities needn't be majorities to prevail, any more than we deferred to majority opinions when we opened our countries to crowds. The very values that opened our countries to others might be the first to fall.

It was evident for years that Asian airlines only hired and retained young, beautiful women to be flight hostesses, before the *News Limited Network* reported an advertisement from a Korean coal company, Pt. Karya Bumi Baratama, for a receptionist in Jakarta in 2013. She had to be "*female, single, max 25 years old,*" and, among other things, "*good looking.*"

"It's a part of their culture," explained Australia InfoMine general manager Johann Robertson. "From what my staff tell me about the South East Asia job region, it really sounds like this receptionist ad in question is looking for the stereotypical demographic for the role that is unencumbered to work longer hours, rather than for any kind of inappropriate relationship."

We recognise different values, when it's a chance to commend other races and think less of ours. The values we know aren't universal are their values better than ours.

When Chinese immigrant Quinghua Pei attempted to bribe a teacher in 2008 to help his son qualify for a selective high school in Sydney, we didn't imagine bribery being an Asian value. Instead, journalist Adele Horin considered education the Asian value. She commended Asians for it.

While we enthuse about Asian values, I read a long time ago that Asian people don't speak of them. There's no Asian monolith, except to the West. Chinese speak of Chinese values, Japanese of Japanese values, and so forth. Multiracial Malaysia speaks of Asian values trying to hold its disparate Asian populations together, much as we talk of universal values trying to hold a universe together.

Our presumptions all people are the same means we attribute differences between countries to political and economic conditions (as we attribute everything to political and economic conditions). We thus conclude immigrants' children will be like ours. They're not.

Outside the West, prisoners in gaols enjoy few or no rights, relying upon their families to bring them food and medicine. Prison officers in China identify prisoners' blood types and other physical features, ready for wealthy Chinese outside gaol requiring healthy kidneys, lungs, hearts, or other organs. The prisoners aren't necessarily sentenced to death and could've been imprisoned for any offence; their releases from gaol might even be imminent. Transplants are carried out as soon as practicable, so healthy organs are often removed from prisoners while they're alive. Anaesthetic is an unnecessary expense.

Sitting comfortably on the rear porch of the Greengate Hotel, my half-Lebanese friend Mark had expected removing organs from live people to horrify every Australian. Among Australians, he counted his friend Geoff: a mortgage broker he called "the money tree" for financing Mark's array of investment houses, home units, and a farm. Geoff had been eager to lend far more money to my wife and me to buy our home than would any bank, far more than we wanted to borrow.

Mark and Geoff shared values around making money, but not rights. Mark said Geoff couldn't see any problem with Chinese prison officers organising organ transplants from prisoners. "He was born in Australia!" exclaimed Mark, as if that should've mattered. Geoff was racially Chinese. "He just says they've lost all their rights by being in gaol!"

The West thinks freedom means the rights of the one, and all ones at that. Other races see freedom as the rights of the many: their many. It's the conflict in meaning between the final scenes of the second Star Trek film, *The Wrath of Khan*, in 1982, and the third, *The Search for Spock*, in 1984. In the former, Spock died to save his friends: the rights of the many outweighed the rights of the one. In the latter, a far more Western tale, Kirk risked everyone's life to find his friend, Spock: the rights of the one (a mixed-species alien) outweighed the rights of the many. At least in that case, the one wasn't a criminal.

Other races' values aren't bad for being different, but they're not ours. I wouldn't dare suggest Western values we hold dear are better than others. Indeed, a sense of some group right, of being a nation and race, is very appealing. Aside from confining wrongdoers to gaol for a time and the death penalty in place in some American states, we have little right to exclude and evict those who could harm us.

Principles underpinning social systems underpin legal systems. We grant not just rights that other races don't, but access to courts and recourse to financial assistance.

We confer upon people facing our criminal courts a presumption of innocence, normally compelling prosecutors to prove an accused's guilt beyond reasonable doubt. The right has become a presumption in the Western mind that people are innocent of all wrongs (even righteous and kind), unless a court of law proves otherwise. Even then, we believe them. We assume asylum seekers and other aspiring immigrants are truthful. (It's not a presumption we grant our forebears or each other with whom we disagree.)

Asians respect authority, at least their own. American criminal court prosecutors prefer Asian jurors, provided the accused isn't Asian. Asian legal systems presume that people charged with crimes are guilty, for otherwise police and prosecutors wouldn't have charged them. The accused must prove his or her innocence.

Presuming that any of our liberties and institutions will remain as we become declining minorities in our countries is presumptuous, if not ludicrous. Being individuals, the changes arising will only bother us if they affect us personally. The most obvious of anything for us relates to money.

We don't protect our people from outsiders, but provide something for them (along with everyone else) materially. Our aged pensions and other benefits are a peculiarly Western phenomenon; other countries don't impose upon their taxpayers the burden of looking after their elderly, sick, and disabled because those people's families look after them. Their relatives continue looking after them when they come to our countries and we give them money, too.

Simply because we've paid taxes to help other races is no reason they should pay taxes to help us. Asians buying wine from my old school friend Stu pay cash, as do Asians paying fees at our sons' high school. They have earned cash without paying the income taxes they're legally obliged to pay.

We have no reason to presume that our model of a state keeping its citizens will endure through our waning lives. Government expenditures providing for elderly white people are already becoming increasingly redirected towards aiding other races; we call it equality. The Western cradle won't always be.

Liberalism has proven incompatible with interracial immigration, as we never imagined when we opened our borders.

No country can remain liberal accommodating people opposed to liberalism.

We individuals don't mind if no countries continue reflecting our values provided we remain true to them, in our shrinking little circles of good-hearted friends. Values lie inside people's heads. Without people to believe them, let alone countries to practice them, they cease to exist. We think we don't need countries because we have our ideals to keep us, until we die in our solitary peace where no one can hear us.

Europeans developed liberalism for sensing the betterment it brought our nations and races. Holding fast to any principle when it's harming our race and nation isn't liberalism. It's ideology.

If we truly treasured freedom and rights, we'd reject racial and religious diversity. We'd enforce our borders from those that don't share our senses of liberty. Liberalism would again be nationalistic.

19. OTHER PEOPLE'S EMPIRES

Europe's colonies have long been beacons to Europeans building nations and bettering their lives. The Americas and Australasia allowed immigration from Europe because we were European, with lesser borders between our own than with other races. America rejected racial segregation in the 1950s and '60s, but countries themselves segregate races behind borders, if they're enforced. Our abodes become beacons for all races wanting better lives, whatever the impact upon us.

At first, it seems governments envisaged few people from other races coming into our countries. (At least, that's what they told us.) We couldn't imagine many people wanting to become racial minorities, but nor did we imagine so many coming that we became minorities. Had we known what would come of our countries half a century on, we'd not have opened our borders as we did.

In America, the Immigration and Nationality Act of 1965 ended the National Origins Formula in place since the Emergency Quota Act of 1921. Among the many supporters of the 1965 bill, Senator Ted Kennedy promised from the Senate floor that "the ethnic mix of this country will not be upset."

It was upset, although one night in 1969, Kennedy showed how little he cared about other white Americans. He left Mary Jo Kopechne to die at Chappaquiddick

A sponsor of the 1965 bill, Senator Eugene McCarthy came to regret the legislation. In 1992, he published *A Colony of the World: The United States Today*. In particular, *"unrecognised by virtually all of the bill's supporters, were provisions which would eventually lead to unprecedented growth in numbers and the transfer of policy control from the elected representatives of the American people to individuals wishing to bring relatives to this country."*

Reverse colonialism turns the old globalisation back to front. Through our age of empires, Western countries were microcosms for what we thought the planet should be. They still are, but we're no longer transforming the world in our image. We're transforming our countries in the world's image. We made our countries lands for the world. We made them available. The end of our colonisation of the world became the world's colonisation of us.

By 1980, Australia's immigration policies were completely indiscriminate but John Menadue, secretary of the Department of Immigration and Ethnic Affairs from then until 1983, had one important qualification. A Sunday newspaper, I think it was, reported his opposition to white South Africans wanting to come because Australia's population was primarily European. (He seems to have imagined the only racist white people left were South African.) Other races could come for their communities here, but not white South Africans. Ours is the globalism of everyone else.

Western governments no longer assume few immigrants will come. We want more. We lose our countries to the colonisers, by the collaboration of our compatriots.

Walking past me on the platform of the Milson's Point railway station, the evening of the last day of August 2010, was a young East Asian man, as there so often is in Sydney. On his black tee shirt was a huge image of red lipstick as kissing lips might leave. Above them was the word, spelt in capital letters and American English: "*COLONIZE.*"

Without us asserting our sovereignty, our lands are open for other races building empires of their own. Asian economic imperialism fosters not immigration but emigration, with none of the shame we feel for our past colonisation. By 2014, the Chinese diaspora numbered forty-eight million worldwide, colonising countries rich and poor. The Overseas Chinese Affairs Office of the State Council oversaw their activities, ensuring their loyalty to China.

The opportunities brought by immigration aren't for the West. They're for everyone else. In 2012, the *Sydney Morning Herald* newspaper's headline 'Changing face of a suburb' enthused about Hurstvillle. Not only were Chinese the dominant race. Those born in mainland China alone were more common than any other race.

Chinese immigration is a boon, but only for Chinese. Justin Wang was selling a hundred apartments a month primarily to young Chinese couples who came to Australia to study, but decided to stay. About a quarter of them received financial help from their parents in China to buy their first home. Naturally enough (although no longer for white people), parents wanted to see their children keep in touch with their racial roots.

Commercial colonialism comes without sense of bringing civilisation, real or imagined. It's running a business. Italian fabric might be the envy of men and women around the world, but two thousand Chinese entrepreneurs owned a quarter of the textile businesses in Prato by 2007, importing cheap Chinese weavers.

In the year to June 2011, China became the leading source of immigrants to Australia. Not only Australian employers complained of labour shortages to justify importing workers. So did China, about labour shortages in Australia. In July 2011, Ouyang Cheng, second secretary for economic and commercial affairs of the Chinese embassy in Australia, said in a speech in Adelaide that China's investment in the country was being hampered by bottlenecks in skilled labour and infrastructure. We took his words as the most natural thing in the world.

China doesn't import workers. It trains its people. We train them too.

Investment from China was a particular focus of the Excellence in Mining & Exploration conference in 2010. The Australian economy was so open and Chinese so organised, Chinese companies wanting to invest in Australia required at most one approval from the compliant Australian Foreign Investment Review Board but three approvals from Chinese authorities, including the Ministry of Commerce.

George Su, managing director of the Silk Road Capital Group, cited the State Administration of Foreign Exchange to say about seventy percent of mainland Chinese money went to Hong Kong. Thus, the innocuous, apparently private money reaching the rest of the world from Hong Kong was really Beijing's. The second and fourth most popular destinations were, as I recall, the Cayman Islands and British Virgin Islands, which meant the rest of the world had no idea what money was coming from Beijing. In third place was Australia.

Late in the second day, the third Tuesday of September, Su was one of two Chinese among the five participants of a panel discussion. The three Australians were no less enthused than the Chinese for China.

Yunnan Copper Resources managing director Jason Beckton

said Chinese companies paid tax on their mineral resources in the ground for being future profits. China thus probably understated its resources. It mined other countries, while keeping resources at home for the future when resources would be fewer. (We can't get our resources out of the ground quick enough, but we don't think of the future.)

Moly Mines chief executive Derek Fisher spoke proudly of all he'd done to facilitate Hanlong buying shares in the company. Chinese companies could source loans much cheaper than could Western companies, at "three hundred to three hundred and fifty points above LIBOR," referring to the London Interbank Offered Rate, an international standard for interest rates. (We mightn't have money, but still have the acronyms.)

The world's largest bank was already the Chinese government-owned Industrial and Commercial Bank of China, whose general manager in Australia was Ruxiang Han. "I think the likelihood of China taking control of Australian resources," he replied to a question about it, "is the same as Imperial China taking Australia as a colony."

In their dark suits, white shirts, and colourful ties, the five men of the panel laughed. So did much of the audience.

"China's public diplomacy is a seamless extension of China's global ambitions for resources and influence," wrote Helle Dale, senior fellow in public diplomacy studies at the Heritage Foundation, in 2010. *"The Western model is increasingly perceived by the Chinese leadership as fatally flawed. Particularly as the world economic crisis takes its toll, the Chinese are making the argument that its state capitalism, the Beijing Consensus, is the way of the future. Obviously this argument has resonance: receptive governments in parts of Africa, Latin America, and Asia want Chinese investment and trade, and the fact that it is delivered without any annoying sermons about democratic reforms or privatisation makes it all the more attractive."*

The rest of the world wants Western money, but not Western political and economic individualism. It wants nationalism.

Other races' empires aren't of ideology as ours have become. They're of race, culture, and nation, where ours used to be.

China Radio International emphasises cultural and informational broadcasting. Chinese are among the world's most aggressive users of student exchange programmes, with the Institute of International Education reporting that more than ninety-eight thousand Chinese students studied in America in 2009.

The Chinese government doesn't just teach children in China. It teaches children in the West, and not only Chinese.

The principal and a teacher at our eldest daughters' high school spent the last week of third term, 2011 at the Hanban headquarters in Beijing to receive their Confucius Classroom Teacher Training. The principal was careful to say, in the preceding school newsletter, that Hanban paid their expenses. *"This session is for school leaders and follows the success Ms Wang has had with Hanban and our students in the Chinese Proficiency contests."*

The Office of Chinese Language Council International in Beijing funds and controls Confucius Institutes promoting the study of Chinese languages and understanding of Chinese culture and business. By 2010, sixty such centres were at American universities and schools. Two hundred and eighty-two were around the world. The Chinese government aimed to fund a thousand.

"On the Confucius Centres," American secretary of state Hillary Clinton told the Senate Foreign Relations Committee in 2010, "the Chinese government provides each centre with a million dollars to launch, plus they cover operating expenses that exceed two hundred thousand dollars per year. We don't have that kind of money in the budget." America spent her money on foreign aid.

The Chinese are taking advantage of the West's rejection of nationalism to spread out, while preventing information and ideas from flowing back to contaminate China. *"Eschewing confrontation,"* wrote Stefan Halper in his 2010 book *The Beijing Consensus, "China's true challenge arises in a separate realm, namely, Beijing's transformative, leading role in the rise of a Chinese brand of capitalism and a Chinese conception of the international community, both opposed to and substantially different from their Western version."*

Sydney University opened its Confucius Institute in 2008. China's consul general remarked that China "would not take kindly" to the institute hosting students or academics opposed to China's policies on Tibet or Falun Gong.

We only fear white people. When the same university, in 2010, allowed the American Australian Association to establish an American studies centre, the *Sydney Morning Herald* declared, 'Sinister role seen in Uni studies centre.'

In an article in the *Australian Universities Review*, political economist Tim Anderson accused Sydney University of sacrificing its academic independence with the American centre. He was particularly concerned about any bias towards America, with only one of the visiting lecturers between 2007 and '09 critical of American foreign policy. (I wondered if anyone critical of China would get within sight of a Confucius Institute.) The university's vice chancellor Michael Spence defended the American centre by, in part, pointing to several academics critical of America.

In 2010, University of Chicago political scientist John Mearsheimer warned that China would seek to dominate Asia over the next thirty years. Its rise would not be peaceful.

From the Australian National University's School of International, Political, and Strategic Studies, retired public servant Stuart Harris rejected Mearsheimer's warning. "The time he is talking about in the next thirty years and his view on China is one of extreme pessimism," said Harris. "There's no doubt China will try to be more active and to some extent dominate in South East Asia, but I don't think they will get to a point where they will outpace the U.S. in that timeframe. The U.S. will be able to keep up."

Western individuals don't think thirty years ahead anyway. We don't think so far as to when there's no longer a West.

Besides, we don't like pessimism. We see merit in optimism. Our vision of a world without borders is predicated upon our unwavering confidence in the kindness of other races, as we don't imagine in our forebears when the empires were ours. We don't mind imperialism, when it's other people's empires.

20. TREASON

I'm not sure any of us learnt anything when our College of Law course in 1986 touched upon ethics, but the debates were good fun. I was twenty-three, turning twenty-four, years old. I knew more about some things then than I know now. About other things, I knew less.

One issue for debate may well have been courts imposing a death penalty upon convicted criminals. The issue had been dealt with too cleverly in my criminal law lectures for me to want the death penalty in Australia in 1986; I suspect few, if any, of us students would have disagreed. The only crimes I imagine anybody contemplated warranting execution were murder and treason, although any debate didn't question that treason should be a criminal offence. Many a Western country gaoled traitors other countries executed.

Among my fellow students was Jill. I didn't know her well, although we'd been in the same rooms of fifteen students in the first and second sections of the course. She was tall, beautiful, blonde-haired, and confident, although confidence was commonplace among the newly graduating lawyers at the college: more commonplace than being tall, beautiful, or blonde. Six or so years earlier, she'd been a student at the prestigious Abbotsleigh College my sisters attended. Jill never seemed particularly political let alone revolutionary, but in response to something I said, in a brief conversation as we left the seminar room, she said of treason: "It shouldn't even be illegal."

Her sentiment surprised me, but brief words meaning nothing to speakers can make listeners question what they'd never before questioned. She'd fobbed off loyalty to any country, not just ours. She had ideals, as we all had ideals, but hers were more important than countries. We were individuals of virtue, we citizens of the world.

From what I knew of Jill, she wasn't leading any cause. It was the only remark I ever heard her make about treason. She expressed what she happened to believe, because it pertained to our conversation. Other students might've said the same thing, if their conversations however brief touched upon treason, but I wasn't privy to another conversation that did.

The West walked away from our lifetime homelands and our ancestral homelands, as no other races have. My multilingual secretary Liz proudly crossed her fingers while taking her oath of loyalty to Her Majesty Queen Elizabeth II for her British citizenship although, having come from Australia, Her Majesty was already her queen.

If we fake our oaths, it beggars belief to imagine immigrants are sincere with theirs. We're cavalier about our commitments, but blithely assume immigrants will honour theirs. Besides, the children of immigrants make no pledges. Difficult as it is to impose conditions on immigrants to live by their host countries' values, it's nigh on impossible to impose conditions on their children, short of being willing to punish or expel them.

We presume citizenship commands devotion from immigrants we don't feel ourselves. With no more evidence than their community spokespeople speaking at microphones, we think our immigrants are loyal to our countries to which we're no longer loyal. We're the ones who opened our borders. Why would immigrants defend our nations we don't? We betray each other and expect immigrants not to betray us, too. Perhaps all we expect of them is that they love indigenous peoples and other immigrants as much as we do.

I recall a television documentary saying Americans of German ancestry, even those born in Germany, were the most passionate of Hollywood's propagandists during the Great War. They proved their patriotism to melting-pot America with films hostile to Germany, but they were fellow North Europeans in a European America that asserted her race and nation. I don't recall the documentary mentioning whether they were Jewish, but suggesting today Jews are loyal more to Zion than their countries of citizenship would be anti-Semitic.

Americans were doubtlessly horrified when American Chinese were prosecuted for treason a few years ago, but quickly assured themselves that most Americans of Chinese and every other ancestry are loyal to America. Anything else would be racist. The Chinese government paid American citizen Ching Ning Guey, a senior manager for the probabilistic risk assessment division of the Tennessee Valley Authority from 2010 until 2014, for sensitive nuclear technological information.

We feel no loyalty to the lands of our forebears, but that's no reason to expect other races not to feel loyalty for theirs. We respect them retaining their histories and ancestries, while we incongruously assume they're not loyal to those histories and ancestries. We presume they can't have been loyal to have left their ancestral lands, but that disregards the incentives we give them to come. People patriotic to their ancestral homelands aren't offering patriotism to their countries of residence if the two ever conflict.

The West presumes more than other races presume, not just for the present but also the past. After the surprise Japanese attack on Pearl Harbour in 1941, the American government didn't insist a hundred thousand Japanese citizens and American Japanese, including American-born citizens, primarily in Hawaii, were loyal Americans contributing so much. Fearing they compromised American security, it interned them. We did many things differently then.

A generation or more later, we rejected nationalist caution. Japan had failed to apologise for launching the war or the atrocities it committed, expressing no more than deep regret in 1984, but that didn't deter America's one hundredth congress in 1987 and President Ronald Reagan in 1988 from apologising and paying reparations for the Japanese internment. They blamed it (in the words of S.1009 from the first session of congress) on racial prejudice, war hysteria, and a failure of political leadership.

In 1941, political leadership meant leaders defending their people and countries. It still does through most of the world. By 1987 in our postmodern West, it meant defending everyone else. Rejecting the will of our race, we call leadership.

Implementing the will of their race, other races call leadership. They enjoy support from their governments, businesses, and peoples. They also enjoy it from ours.

Hungry for Chinese investment, West Australian premier Colin Barnett blamed frostiness in the relationship between China and Australia in 2009 squarely on the Australian government. He later publicly contemplated appointing China the defence force for an independent Western Australia.

Without nations of our own, we imagine belonging with others.

In 2012, Australian businessman James Packer accorded Australia a national identity completely subservient to China. "We," he said, "as a country, have to try harder to let China know how grateful we are for their business."

What we don't sell, we give away. Australian businessman Kerry Stokes wanted China's interests to determine Australian taxation and defence policies. He said the mining tax was a "dreadful and wrong message to our Chinese friends." American troops in Australia "physically repulsed" him.

We've moved beyond individualism to counter-nationalism. None of those Australians complained when China re-imposed tariffs upon imported coal in 2014, collecting more money than Australia collected from the mining tax (by then revoked) and costing Australian jobs.

More than simply discarding our national interests, we actively oppose them. Western businesspeople cuddling up to foreigners for a few more pieces of silver express the same contempt for their countries as their children carrying placards welcoming refugees.

Treason is no longer an offence. It's a right.

Our homelands being ours, with our peoples co-operating, is nationalism. Without it, we can spend forever pursuing places in which to belong, never finding them among other races.

21. DISPOSSESSION

When other races came to our neighbourhoods, we welcomed them, but our lives deteriorated. Sooner or later, we moved away. The phrase "white flight" describes the people who fled those streets, suburbs, and cities across America and Britain. New South Wales education minister John Della Bosca shouted the phrase down for being racist when applied to Sydney schools in 2008.

His federal counterpart Julia Gillard was no more forgiving. "Part of growing up and part of being an adult in Australia today," she told Australian parents, "is you've got to have the abilities to mix in multicultural Australia."

"This school has put off Anglo-Saxon white people from attending because they have become the minority," responded one anonymous parent, "and the other Asian children do not want to associate with them because they have their own types, and also because they don't speak the language."

Shaun, a colleague of mine at Cement Australia, once mentioned his surprise to hear of racist abuse of a player in his beloved rugby union. "People don't think like that anymore," he said. Well, we don't.

A decade later, the first Tuesday in May 2014, I came across Shaun again in our local supermarket. He and his wife were looking to move away from the home in which they'd raised their children, because the suburb was becoming Chinese. "If I'd wanted to live in Hong Kong," he told me, "I'd have moved there."

"Immigration's been good for us," said my former Holyman Limited colleague Peter C, in the lounge bar at the Art House Hotel the third Tuesday of April 2010. Again we sat with glasses of beer, this time Heineken, in front of us.

"Why?" I asked him.

"The restaurants," answered Peter.

"Every time anyone says they like immigration, it's for the food."

"That's right."

We don't need immigration for food. Our chefs can prepare the cuisines of other cultures and races, if we want them. Chefs outside the West prepare and serve Western foods, without immigration.

Peter liked seeing a wealthy suburb like Killara becoming Chinese: altering and demolishing the old homes that could have been his heritage if we weren't so divided by class. I went onto tell him of the Australian managing director of Golden Cross Resources Limited welcoming a Chinese takeover of the country.

"Is he mad?" asked Peter. There was a limit to Peter's acceptance of what was happening, after all. "He should be taken out and shot!"

Not only white people flee places when we're no longer the majority. Rob had been my friend since childhood when, in the 1990s, he and his Indian wife Junean moved from Granville in Sydney. They wanted their mixed-race daughter to sit in a school where most children were white.

We're still giving rights to the rest of the world, even when our lives aren't so good anymore. We've decided the West wasn't ours to begin with. By the twenty-first century, the people we see are as likely as not to be Asians at work and Africans not.

In April 2010, demographers Macroplan forecast the Australian-born family would be a minority by 2025. "It all adds to the cosmopolitan nature of modern Australia," enthused KPMG demographer Bernard Salt, although the country already housed every race. He can only have meant the fewer white people, the more cosmopolitan a country. All those racially homogenous countries without any white people must be very cosmopolitan.

His sense of Australia, of who we are, moved effortlessly between races (without acknowledging the traditional owners), blithely assuming we're Australians of whatever race. "It means our views become less blinkered," he continued, "and we become more tolerant, confident, engaged, opportunistic and optimistic because we are open to new ideas, not obsessed with keeping things the same."

In fact, white Australia was never obsessed with keeping things the same. We were confident, engaged, opportunistic, and optimistic, at least until 1914 (and for a while there in the 1950s and '60s), as other races now are. We're *more* blinkered and *less* tolerant than we used to be, about some things. We applaud the changes we claim immigrant races brought in forty years, while applauding Aborigines for not changing in forty thousand.

We fail to distinguish individuals from groups, as other races do. We don't appreciate the possibility of restricting citizenship to our race, while allowing our friends from other races to live by us. That option doesn't exist.

My life is better because my friends Ted, Karthik, and Humphrey (who does work) came to Australia from Hong Kong, India, and Africa. My life is better for Jews like my friends Gregor, Ian Biner, and Julian and two Jews I called my uncles. In spite of my friends and uncles from other races, my life would be better if we'd only allowed our race to immigrate, because then I'd have a community and country.

Most, if not all, instances of friendships between races arise where the dominant race is Western. We're more likely to befriend a black man among the predominantly white leaders of our local cub scout pack than in Harlem, New York.

Divisions between races were supposed to fade away over time, but the more people of other races have come to Australia, the fewer friends I have among them. Understandably, they'd rather spend time with their race. They now have more chance to do so.

Western interests are individual. Immigrants' interests are also those of their families and race. They come to craft better lives for them and their children, as we no longer imagine. We share what we have with them, rather than keeping it for our children.

When I was young, parents spoke to their children of how much harder life had been for them through the Great Depression, World War II, and its aftermath than it was for us. I'd love to be able to say the same to my children: that our accumulating wealth and technologies will make their lives better than mine has been, as the immigrants can say to their children. I can't. Life is harder now, and it's harder because we're giving away our children's inheritance. We advance other races at their expense.

Dedicated coaching colleges after school, at weekends, and in school holidays, along with family support and focus on rote learning, offer Asian children courses and careers that could have been our children's. No longer able to rely upon their intellect and abilities with time also to play, my children study more than I studied to achieve less than I did. In their second last year of school, my eldest son missed his friend Michael's birthday party to study. Michael called him "a white Asian" for studying so much.

We don't discriminate to save our sacrificial children, let alone our compatriots' children. Defending them, we call xenophobic.

By 2010, ninety-five percent of students listed a language background other than English in their entry applications for New South Wales' top selective school, James Ruse Agricultural High School. Children of immigrants filled almost eighty percent of places offered at the state's top ten selective high schools. Chinese dominated, followed by Vietnamese and Koreans. A director of the Centre for Population and Urban Research at Monash University, Bob Birrell, said the successful students largely represented middle-class and upper middle-class families from Asia, who emphasised education and professional achievement.

Birrell's words were still in my mind the day after I'd read them, as I stood talking with a middle-aged parishioner at my Baptist church. It was Anzac Day 2010, but we didn't talk of the soldiers who fought and died. (There wasn't any point.) Instead, she talked of the many nationalities of people she'd befriended in the street in which she lived, Toolang Road. Among her neighbours she helped was a child. "You know what the Chinese are like," she said, before quickly explaining. "He's Chinese." She hadn't previously mentioned the boy's race. "Always got their heads in the books, day and night."

I toyed with telling her that what she'd said was illegal, as much for the fun of it as anything else, but complimenting other races isn't illegal. She certainly hadn't intended to vilify them.

The television programme *A Current Affair* of the seventh of November 2012 reported a Castle Hill shopping centre removing Australian shopkeepers to target the suburb's Asian population. The Australian Communications and Media Authority ruled that the report breached three clauses of the Commercial Television Industry Code of Practice. The report contained "inaccurate factual material," by saying the centre would be *all* Asian. It placed "a gratuitous emphasis on ethnic origin," as if the shopping centre hadn't. The programme shouldn't have reported the story, being likely to "provoke intense dislike and serious contempt on the grounds of ethnic origin." We can only mention other races to applaud them.

Pauline Hanson was back in the news (as she'd rarely been out of it) for being a candidate in the 2011 New South Wales election. *"I still fondly remember her 1996 maiden speech about the dangers of Asians swamping Australia,"* gloated homosexual Benjamin Law, in a long open letter to the people of the state. *"Retrieve it online and you'll also have a very good chuckle, though that could just be reflux. 'They have their own culture and religion, form ghettos and do not assimilate,' she said about Asians — which is to say, me and my people."*

When homosexual white people talk of their people, they mean other homosexuals. When homosexuals of other races speak of their people, they mean their race.

"15 years later and we know she was wrong, of course. Not necessarily about the swamping thing (seriously, look around: our takeover is almost complete), but the idea that people actually care."

Law was cocky. He was also correct. The open West is very different for him and his people than it is for me and mine. They're gaining countries. We're losing ours. Asians wouldn't tolerate being swamped in their countries.

We commiserate, even cry, for Aborigines, Maori, and American Indians feeling pains of dispossession from the lands of their birth. We mock our race feeling the same.

Writing about a demonstration against the Australian government's proposed carbon tax the penultimate Wednesday of March 2011, journalist Bernard Keane made no end of disparaging generalisations by race: his own. *"What was interesting about the crowd wasn't so much its average age – 60, at least… – but its colour,"* he wrote. *"This was a monocultural crowd, overwhelmingly Anglo-Celtic in the old phrase."* (That was the phrase in between being Australian and disappearing altogether.)

The demonstration, wrote Keane, wasn't *"really about climate change or immigration, but about social change and the social and economic transformation of Australia in a way that older, white Australians resent. This crowd grew up in a monocultural, British country that relied on protected industries – particularly the 'real jobs' to be found in manufacturing. They grew up with a political system dominated by old white men. Australia has changed beyond recognition for them and because of their education levels and their age, they aren't as well equipped to handle it as others are."* (If Keane wasn't presuming they were uneducated, he was dismissing their education out of hand.) *"They therefore feel disoriented, dispossessed and resentful, particularly because they don't hold the same pre-eminent position they used to hold socially, economically or politically."*

A similar view to Keane's came from Barack Obama during the American presidential election campaign of 2008, while addressing wealthy supporters in San Francisco. He wasn't dismissing his race, but ours. "It's not surprising, then," said Obama of old and poor white Americans who continued supporting Hillary Clinton for the Democratic Party nomination, "they get bitter, they cling to guns or religion or antipathy to people who aren't like them or anti-immigrant sentiment or anti-trade sentiment as a way to explain their frustrations."

Obama said later that he regretted his choice of words, but no one seemed to question his presumptions about problem white people. Much like our indigenous peoples, they've not gone anywhere, but they're feeling like intruders to the lands in which they, their parents, and their grandparents were born. We've become strangers, but when those left alone don't celebrate aloneness, we throw them further aside.

They're white folk: our pejorative way to describe our race. We mention them to malign them for not welcoming the loss of their countries: for hanging onto ideas of having countries. They're dispossessed from the nations their forebears founded and built. They're the malcontents reticent about becoming racial minorities, who contemplate any negativity about it. To be a postmodern white person is to be buffeted back and forth, unwanted outside the West and within, without anywhere to feel secure. They're old-fashioned, stupid, unable to cope.

When other races feel demoted, we're so quick to care. We sympathise for immigrants feeling unwelcome, although they voluntarily undertook the changes in their lives, improving their lives, and in their new homes are in growing communities.

We offer our race none of the sympathy we afford indigenous races. We demand empathy for other races' experiences, but don't try to comprehend our compatriots' fears. We don't imagine the lives that they've lived: their nationalism giving them ownership of nations we've stripped from them, without their choosing. We torment our race feeling disenfranchised from the only homes they've known.

When white people question immigration, we rarely change our policies. We change our people.

To deal with their anxieties about immigration in 2011 and '12, the American Department of Agriculture required its employees to attend cultural sensitivity training programmes. Department secretary Tom Vilsack described them in a memorandum as a "*new era of Civil Rights*" and "*a broader effort towards cultural transformation at USDA.*"

The department paid diversity awareness trainer and self-described "citizen of the world" mixed-race Samuel Betances almost two hundred thousand dollars to tell employees what to believe, forcing them to repeat it. "I want you to say that American was founded by outsiders, say that," he told them, "who are today's insiders, who are very nervous about today's outsiders. I want you to say, 'The pilgrims were illegal aliens.' Say, 'The pilgrims never gave their passports to the Indians.'"

The employees chanted those words.

"Give me a bam!" Betances told them.

The audience did so in unison.

"By the way," asked Betances at one point, "I don't like the word 'minorities.' How about 'emerging majorities?'" Presumably that meant white Americans should be called emerging minorities.

Nazi and communist rallies never had anything on Western cultural sensitivity training. The Jonestown cult might have come close by 1978, shortly before its mass suicide.

Democracy becomes not so much "government of the people, by the people, for the people," in Abraham Lincoln's words, but "people of the government, by the government, for the government." Our values aren't the masters of government, but the servants. Were Western governments representing their people, they'd alleviate their anxieties. That would be nationalism.

Among the people wanting countries in which to belong are many of us doing personally well. (My little life is terrific.) We simply feel what other races feel: collective connections to the lands of our forebears and birth. We care for our children and race, rather than succumbing to Western individualism.

Nationalists care for their compatriots. Globalists care only for themselves: their visions of their individual selves.

We alone opened our countries to all comers, to the point of losing what we had. No other races concede what we're conceding. We've lost our lands to belong.

White people don't normally riot (except over sport), but there surely can be no better antidote to prejudice than to free people from fear. A moratorium on unilateral immigration could make life easier for immigrants already in the West by reducing white people's angst and insecurity. If Western races felt less under threat, there could be peace of mind. Were other races losing as much by their governments' hands as we're losing, there'd be revolution. In Fiji, there was, several times over.

BIBLIOGRAPHY, REFERENCES

Articles

Ahmed, Tanveer, 'Knock, knock, who's there? Hopeful souls at every door,' *The Sydney Morning Herald* newspaper, 14 November 2009.

Alexander, Harriet, 'Sydney is China's new friend,' *The Sydney Morning Herald* newspaper, 18 June 2008, reporting on the opening of the Confucius Institute at the University of Sydney. Heath Gilmore, 'Sinister role seen in uni studies centre,' *The Sydney Morning Herald* newspaper, 22 September 2010, concerning the American studies centre.

Benson, Simon, 'Most asylum seekers to Australia dump their passports,' *The Daily Telegraph* newspaper, 7 May 2011.

Berg, Chris, 'Memo to unions: White Australia was a bad idea,' *The Sydney Morning Herald* newspaper, 6 November 2011.

Bissett, Kelvin, 'Australia throwing out the human trash,' *The Daily Telegraph* newspaper, 18 June 2008. Uncredited, 'Pedophile Raymond Horne sent back to UK,' *Australian Associated Press* news service, 21 March 2008. Adele Horin, 'Minister urged to stop deportation of NZ woman,' *The Sydney Morning Herald* newspaper, 24 December 2007. Sue Hewitt, 'Decision to kick a convicted sexual predator out of Australia is overturned,' *Sunday Herald Sun* newspaper, 5 September 2010.

Braithwaite, Alyssa, 'Fraser sorry for racist refugee remarks,' *Australian Associated Press* news service, 30 August 2006. Tim Dick, 'Uni suspends outspoken academic,' *The Sydney Morning Herald* newspaper, 30 July 2005. Andrew Fraser's statement responding to the vice chancellor was published in *The Sydney Morning Herald* newspaper, 29 July 2005.

Brown, Malcolm, 'Indigenous jobs are focus for new Uluru resort owners,' *The Sydney Morning Herald* newspaper, 28 May 2011.

Burke, Jason and others, 'All Australia can offer is guano island,' *The Observer* newspaper, 2 September 2001. Uncredited, 'Asia doesn't judge us on asylum seekers, says Carr,' *The Sydney Morning Herald* newspaper, 28 January 2003.

Burke, Liz, 'Palmer United Party Senator Zhenya 'Dio' Wang says Tiananmen was 'the right thing to do',' *News Limited Network*, 9 June 2015.

Burton-Bradley, Robert and Paul Kelly, 'China expert says academics claims China will 'dominate' in the next 30 years 'pessimistic',' *Agence France-Presse* news service published at *News Limited Network*, 3 August, 2010.

Butler, Patrick, 'Millions of Britons unable to cope with modern life, says study,' *The Guardian* newspaper, 7 December 2009.

Chrisafis, Angelique, 'Anti-racism group targets Louvre,' *The Guardian* newspaper, published in *The Sydney Morning Herald* newspaper, 29 May 2009.

Cleland, Gary, 'Sainsbury's says 'immigrants better workers',' *The Telegraph* newspaper, 9 October 2007.

Colford, Paul, "Illegal immigrant' no more,' *Associated Press* news service, 2 April 2014. Bianca Hall, 'Minister wants boat people called illegals,' *The Sydney Morning Herald* newspaper, 20 October 2013.

Coorey, Phillip, 'Thomson turns his back on Labor,' *The Sydney Morning Herald* newspaper, 1 November 2012.

Daily Mail reporter, 'School defends experiment to separate black students in a bid to boost their academic results,' *Daily Mail* newspaper, 17 January 2011.

Dawber, Alistair, 'Israel gave birth control to Ethiopian Jews without their consent,' *The Independent* newspaper, 27 January 2013. Uncredited, 'Netanyahu: African migrants could overrun Israel,' *Associated Press* news service, 20 May 2012.

De Brito, Sam, 'Getting real about racism,' *The Sydney Morning Herald* newspaper, 30 May 2013.

Duff, Eamonn, 'St John's patron in racial outrage,' *The Sydney Morning Herald* newspaper, 11 November 2012.

Ergas, Henry, 'More migrants yes, but weigh the risks,' *The Australian* newspaper, 16 August 2010.

Farmer, Richard, 'Picking on the foreigners,' *Crikey* website, 19 November 2010.

Fitzgerald, Jim, 'Residents get 6 votes each in suburban NY election,' *Associated Press* news service published at *Yahoo! News*, 15 June 2010. Uncredited, 'Hispanic apparent winner in unusual Hudson Valley election,' *Associated Press* news service, 16 June 2010.

Gallagher, Heather and Susan Murdoch, 'Shut away and forgotten, Elsie Brown died alone,' *The Age* newspaper, 15 March 2003.

Gardner, Nick, 'We'll be a nation of new migrants,' *The Sunday*

Telegraph newspaper, 18 April 2010. Uncredited, 'Big fall in migrant arrivals – 32 per cent fall in the past year,' *The Sunday Telegraph* newspaper, 12 September 2010.

Gittins, Ross, 'Punters well aware of economic case against more immigration,' *The Sydney Morning Herald* newspaper, 24 November 2010. Ross Gittins, 'Stop beating about the bush and talk about Big Australia,' *The Sydney Morning Herald* newspaper, 4 August 2010.

Green, Shane, 'Africans having to fight against 'history of failure on blackness',' *The Age* newspaper, 26 April, 2011.

Grossman, Ron, 'Jewish voters don't reflexively back Rahm Emanuel for Chicago mayor,' *The Chicago Tribune* newspaper, 3 October 2010.

Han, Esther, 'Chinese Australians call for an apology,' *The Sydney Morning Herald* newspaper, 30 June 2011. Uncredited, 'City of Sydney officially declares 1788 settlement of Australia an invasion,' *The Daily Telegraph* newspaper, 28 June 2011.

Hartcher, Peter, 'Puff for magic dragon ignores China's fragility,' *The Sydney Morning Herald* newspaper, 18 September, 2012.

Henderson, Gerard, 'Media's soft treatment of Brown opens door to the little Greens men,' *The Sydney Morning Herald* newspaper, 3 April 2012.

Hendley, Matthew, 'Jose Zarate Killed Woman for Not Letting Him Date Her 13-Year-Old Daughter, MCSO Says,' *Phoenix New Times* newspaper, 4 April 2013. Staff report, 'MCSO: Mother killed after she denies man romantic access to underage daughter,' *FOX 10 News Phoenix*, 2 April 2013.

Hepworth, Annabel, 'Business leaders say we need boatpeople,' *The Australian* newspaper, 6 August 2010.

Horin, Adele, 'Asian values are no bad thing in the classroom,' *The Sydney Morning Herald* newspaper, 13 December 2008.

Horin, Adele, 'Fewer volunteers in migrant suburbs,' *The Sydney Morning Herald* newspaper, 11 February 2008.

Hurst, Daniel, "Immigration levels can go up': Labor leadership hopeful Bill Shorten outlines his vision on Q&A,' *The Sydney Morning Herald* newspaper, 1 October 2013.

Hutcheon, Stephen, 'More ceremony fakes unearthed,' *The Sydney Morning Herald* newspaper, 15 August 2008, concerning the Beijing Olympic Games.

Irvine, Jessica, 'Rental crisis linked to migration boom,' *The Sydney*

Morning Herald newspaper, 25 September 2008.

Jones, Gemma, 'Accused killer released on visa and free to work,' *The Daily Telegraph* newspaper, 21 September 2012.

Judicial Watch Press Room, 'JW Releases Confidential USDA Videos Revealing 'Cultural Sensitivity Training' Program,' *Judicial Watch*, 14 February 2013.

Kasolowsky, Raissa and Lin Noueihed, 'Beach sex trial highlights Dubai cultural divide,' *Reuters India* news service, 24 September 2008.

Keane, Bernard, 'Placards not the only thing on display as the denialists gather,' *Crikey* website, 24 March 2011.

Kelleher, Jennifer, 'Not all born in American Samoa want US citizenship,' *Associated Press* news service, 9 February 2020, also reporting on the Northern Mariana Islands.

Keller, Bill, 'Gorbachev Urges Minority States,' *The New York Times* newspaper, 18 April 1987.

Kirkup, James, 'Head of the OBR Robert Chote expands on their long-standing assessment that Britain needs a steady flow of migrant labour to fund public services in the coming decades,' *The Telegraph* newspaper, 14 January 2014.

Kuebler, Martin, 'Swiss voters approve harsher deportation plan,' *Deutsche Welle*, 28 November 2010.

Lee Kuan Yew, interviewed by Hans Hoyng and Andreas Lorenz, "It's Stupid to be Afraid," *Der Spiegel* magazine, 8 August, 2005.

Lloyd, Jonathan, 'Governor Signs Bill Allowing Driver's Licenses for Undocumented Immigrants,' *NBC Los Angeles News*, 3 October 2013. Noreen O'Donnell, 'Illegal immigrants allowed to practice law in California,' *Reuters* news service, 5 October 2013.

Marszalek, Jessica, 'Indonesia's death-row double standard,' *News Limited Network*, 6 May 3013.

Masters, Emma and staff, 'Chinese asylum seekers take Australian option,' *Australian Broadcasting Corporation News*, 11 April 2012. Philip Wen, 'Chinese lured with 'buy land and migrate' pitch,' *The Sydney Morning Herald* newspaper, 11 April 2012.

May, Caroline, 'Study: Net Job Growth in NC Since 2000 Went to Immigrants,' *Breitbart News*, 2 September 2014.

McDonald, Hamish, 'One Korea, one enormous challenge,' *The Sydney Morning Herald* newspaper, 30 July 2011.

McKelway, Bill, 'Illegal alien in nun's traffic death had offenses handled inconsistently,' *Richmond Times-Dispatch* newspaper, 4

March 2011. Staff writers, 'Man charged with killing nun in Virginia car crash is illegal immigrant,' *The Washington Times* newspaper published in *News Core*, 3 August 2010.

Media Release, 'Free swimming lessons for overseas-born adults,' *Ku-ring-gai Council*, 19 March 2015.

Miller, Barbara, 'Migrants drown after boats capsize near island of Samos off coast of Greece,' *Australian Broadcasting Corporation News* and *Agence France-Presse* news service at *Australian Broadcasting Corporation News*, 6 May 2014.

Morri, Mark with Evin Priest, 'Lawless Australian thugs copy mayhem of US organised crime groups,' *The Daily Telegraph* newspaper, 14 February 2011, referring to Afghans.

Murphy, Padraic, 'No going back to Lebanon after ex-wife reveals secret to man's family,' *Herald Sun* newspaper, 26 August 2011.

Navarrette, Ruben, 'Mexican Elites Secretly Agree with Donald Trump,' *The Daily Beast*, 6 July 2015.

Newton, Jennifer, 'Convicts to be referred to as 'justice-involved individuals' by Department of Justice in bid to improve their chances of finding work and a home,' *Daily Mail* newspaper, 28 April 2016.

Ni, Ching-Ching, "Birthing tourism' center in San Gabriel shut down,' *Los Angeles Times* newspaper, 25 March 2011.

Nicholls, Sean and Matt Wade, 'Sydney should embrace Asia, says O'Farrell,' *The Sydney Morning Herald* newspaper, 7 November 2011. Andrew West, 'Vibrant suburbs offer more comfort for new migrants,' *The Sydney Morning Herald* newspaper, 8 November 2011.

O'Rourke, Jim, 'Changing face of a suburb,' *The Sydney Morning Herald* newspaper.

Owen, Glen, 'US shock jock Savage targeted 'to balance least wanted list,' *Daily Mail* newspaper, 25 July 2009. Uncredited, 'US 'hate list' DJ to sue Britain,' *BBC News*, 6 May 2009.

Patty, Anna, 'State ministers warned of flight from schools,' *The Sydney Morning Herald* newspaper, 11 March, 2008.

Patty, Anna and Andrew Stevenson, 'Top school's secret weapon: 95% of students of migrant heritage,' *The Sydney Morning Herald* newspaper, 13 September 2010.

Pollard, Chris, 'John Cleese: London is no longer English city,' *The Sun* newspaper, 3 September 2011, with comment by Kensmith. Miriam Shaviv, 'Candidate Ken's attitude to Jews may be key in race to run London,' *Jewish Times* newspaper, 27 April 2012 mentioned Boris Johnson's great-grandfathers.

Power, Ben, 'Unleashed: Rudd's immigration policy doesn't add up,' *Australian Broadcasting Corporation News*, 12 August 2008.

Preston, Julia, 'Thousands Rally Nationwide in Support of an Immigration Overhaul,' *The New York Times* newspaper, 6 October 2013.

Probyn, Andrew and Nick Butterly, 'Better life main reason for refugees' journey,' *The Sydney Morning Herald* newspaper, 4 May 2011.

Ryan, Peter and staff, 'Business group calls for immigration increase to 220,000,' *Australian Broadcasting Corporation News*, 13 January 2014.

Salt, Bernard, 'Migrants key to replacing baby boomers,' *The Australian* newspaper, 1 October 2009.

Salter, Frank, 'The Misguided Advocates of Open Borders,' *Quadrant* magazine, June 2010.

Satterfield, Jamie, 'Ex-nuke manager admits Chinese paid him for secrets,' *Knoxville (Tenn.) News Sentinel* published at *USA Today Network*, 29 April 2016.

Scicluna, Chris, 'Malta to sell citizenship to foreigners,' *Reuters* news service published in *The Age* newspaper, 13 November 2013.

Sheehan, Paul, 'The Yarra monster is killing us,' *The Sydney Morning Herald* newspaper, 23 August 2010. Tim Colebatch, 'Growing pains: Victoria's population explosion,' *The Age* newspaper, 20 November 2010.

Shorten, Kristin, 'Mining company seeks good looking receptionist in controversial job ad,' *News Limited Network*, 20 March 2013.

Spielmann, Peter James, 'Carter: If no Palestine, Israel sees 'catastrophe',' *Associated Press* news service, 26 January 2009.

Stack, Liam, 'Yale's Halloween Advice Stokes a Racially Charged Debate,' *The New York Times* newspaper, 8 November 2015.

Stolz, Greg, 'Gold Coast judge backs New Zealand man's claim of 'de facto' Australian status,' *The Courier Mail* newspaper, 12 February 2011.

Stone, John, 'Immigration Policy: Our Self-Inflicted Wounds,' *Quadrant* magazine, Volume LIV, Number 9, September 2010.

Strong, Geoff, 'Olympian steps up to grapple for Higgins,' *The Sydney Morning Herald* newspaper, 5 November 2009.

Tanner, Lindsay, 2008 Redmond Barry Lecture, *State Library of*

Victoria.

Totaro, Paola, 'Recession fuels fear of foreigners and lurch to right,' *The Sydney Morning Herald* newspaper, headed 'Migrants blamed as economic crisis in Europe bites' in *The Age* newspaper, 28 September 2010.

Traynor, Ian, 'Gaddafi wants $7b to stem migration,' *The Guardian News & Media* published at *The Sydney Morning Herald* newspaper, 3 September 2010. Martin Bendeler, 'Gaddafi's guards steal from African refugees as they flee Libya,' *Crikey* website, 21 April 2011. Andrea Vogt, 'Italy violated human rights by returning migrants to Libya, court rules,' *The Guardian* newspaper, 23 February 2012. Uncredited, 'Italy migrant boat disaster due to crackdown, says United Nations official,' *Agence France-Presse* news service published at *The Sydney Morning Herald* newspaper, 4 October 2013.

Tully, Meg, 'Md. House passes bill allowing illegal immigrants in-state tuition,' *The Frederick News-Post* newspaper, 8 April 2011. Uncredited, 'House approves lowering tuition for Colorado illegal immigrant students, bill goes to governor,' *ABC 7 News Denver*, 8 March 2013.

Uncredited, 'Accused murderer given bridging visa, says immigration department official,' *Australian Associated Press* news service published at *News Limited Network*, 27 May 2013.

Uncredited, 'Australia a magnet for banker 'refugees',' *Reuters* news service, 1 June 2008.

Uncredited, 'Business booms as old Ashfield becomes new Shanghai,' *The Sydney Morning Herald* newspaper, 18 June 2011.

Uncredited, 'Canada to appeal asylum for S African,' *Agence France-Presse* news service published in *The Sydney Morning Herald* newspaper, 4 September 2009. Maygene de Wee, 'Huntley's wife 'livid' with him,' *News 24*, 9 September 2009. SAPA, 'Huntley's refugee status overturned,' *News 24*, 26 November 2010.

Uncredited, 'Car kills eight cyclists in horror smash in Italy,' *Associated Press* news service, 6 December 2010.

Uncredited, 'Chinese migrants top Britons for first time,' *Bloomberg* news service published at *The Sydney Morning Herald* newspaper, 10 August 2011.

Uncredited, 'Convicted boat race protester wins fight against deportation from Britain,' *Australian Broadcasting Corporation*

News, 10 December 2013, "He is a victim': Puneet Puneet's family won't challenge fugitive son's extradition,' *The Sydney Morning Herald* newspaper, 9 December 2013.

Uncredited, 'Dalai Lama says 'Europe belongs to Europeans, *The Business Times* newspaper, 13 September 2018.

Uncredited, 'England centre is the next Sonny Bill, says Jonny Wilkinson,' *Agence France-Presse* news service. *The Sydney Morning Herald* newspaper introduced the article from the front page of its website with the words *"From illegal immigrant to the next Sonny Bill,"* 4 September 2011.

Uncredited, 'Ethnic-Based Scouting in the Australian Context,' *Scouting in NSW*, Winter/Spring 2011.

Uncredited, 'From the jungle to Cowra's winter,' *Sun Herald* newspaper, 21 December 2008.

Uncredited, 'Govt rejects call to cut immigration,' *The West Australian* newspaper and *Australian Associated Press* news service, 20 February 2009.

Uncredited, 'Hispanic Custodians on Auraria Campus Claim Discrimination,' *CBS 4 Denver*, 9 May 2013.

Uncredited, 'Illegal Immigrant: Reports in Central America Encourage Trek North,' *KRGV News*, 3 June 2014.

Uncredited, 'Immigration 'small benefit' to UK,' *BBC News*, 1 April 2008.

Uncredited, 'Japan to Deport Chinese 'Economic Refugees',' *The New York Times* newspaper, 12 September 1989.

Uncredited, 'Judge 'sought sex from refugee',' *News Core*, 24 February 2010.

Uncredited, 'Liberal candidate attacked in SA: report,' *Australian Associated Press* news service published in *The Sydney Morning Herald* newspaper, 17 July 2010. Uncredited, 'Liberal candidate hit in the head,' *Australian Associated Press* news service published at *News Limited Network*, 17 July 2010.

Uncredited, 'Merkel: Germany is becoming a 'country of immigration',' *Deutsche Welle*, 1 June 2015.

Uncredited, 'More than faces in the crowd,' *The Sydney Morning Herald* newspaper, 23 June 2012.

Uncredited, 'Obama: 'Bitter' comments were ill chosen,' *Associated Press* news service published in *USA Today* newspaper, 4 April 2008.

Uncredited, 'Obama: Being American is 'not a matter of blood or birth',' *The New York Post* newspaper, 1 July 2011.

Uncredited, 'PLO official: Palestinians, Israelis must be totally separated,' *Haaretz* newspaper citing *USA Today*, 14 September 2011. *"Haaretz.com provides extensive and in-depth coverage of…Jewish life in Israel and the Diaspora."*

Uncredited, 'Prosecutors reveal DSK's 'brief' sex with maid probably not consensual but she repeatedly lied,' *Agence France-Presse* news service published in *The Sydney Morning Herald* newspaper, 23 August 2011.

Uncredited, 'Protests at Nigerian's 'murder',' *Kathimerini*, available with the *International Herald Tribune* newspaper in Greece and Cyprus, 21 August 2007.

Uncredited, 'Refugees 'forced into sub-standard housing',' *Australian Broadcasting Corporation News*, 7 December 2010.

Uncredited, 'Report slams Malaysia's refugee record,' *The Sydney Morning Herald* newspaper, 17 June 2010.

Uncredited, 'Saudi princess wins asylum in Britain,' *The Sydney Morning Herald* newspaper and *Agence France-Presse* news service, 20 July 2009.

Uncredited, 'Sugar slaves black chapter in agricultural history,' *Australian Broadcasting Corporation Rural News*, 27 September 2013.

Viellaris, Renee, 'Dole payment plan for illegal migrants,' *Courier Mail* newspaper, 25 June 2008.

Watson, Paul Joseph, 'UC Professor: Immigration Influx is About 'Re-Education' of Society,' *Alex Jones' Infowars*, 25 June 2014.

Weisser, Rebecca, 'Hirsi Ali urges refugee testing,' *The Australian* newspaper, 26 July 2010.

Whitehead, Tom, 'Opponents of immigration could be racist, warned advisers a decade ago,' *The Telegraph* newspaper, 23 February 2010. Tim Shipman, 'Immigrants? We sent out search parties to get them to come… and made it hard for Britons to get work, says Mandelson,' *Daily Mail* newspaper, 14 May 2013.

Winter, Jana, 'Calif. College Offers Scholarship to Illegal Immigrants,' *Fox News*, 28 May 2010.

Young, Ian writing as the Hongcouver, 'Born in China, Joy Mo blames rich mainlanders for Vancouver's housing woes,' *South China Morning Post* newspaper, 4 December 2013.

Books, Letters, and Pamphlets

Beck, Roy, *The Case Against Immigration: The moral, economic, social, and environmental reasons for reducing U.S. immigration back to traditional levels* (1996), WW Norton & Company, Inc.

Boswell, James, 1740-1795, *The Life of Samuel Johnson, LL.D.* (1791), entry for Friday 7 April 1775, quoting Samuel Johnson, 1709-1784.

Cloud, Henry, born 1956, and John Townsend, born 1952, *Boundaries: When to Say Yes, How to Say No to Take Control of Your Life* (1992).

Fraser, Malcolm, 1930-2015, and Margaret Simons, *Malcolm Fraser: The Political Memoirs* (2010), Miegunyah Press, quoted in a *Crikey* daily mail.

Herzl, Theodor, 1860-1904, *Der Judenstaat (The Jewish State): Attempt at a Modern Solution to the Jewish Question* (1896), a pamphlet.

Jiann Hua To, James, *Qiaowu: Extra-Territorial Policies for the Overseas Chinese* (2014), summarised in *The Wall Street Journal* newspaper, 16 August 2014. Andrew Browne, 'The Great Chinese Exodus,' *The Wall Street Journal* newspaper, 15 August 2014. Peter Kwong, 'Chinese Migration Goes Global: Migrants from the world's most populous nation influence more than 150 countries,' *Yale Global*, 17 July 2007.

Judaken, Jonathan, born 1968, *Jean-Paul Sartre and the Jewish Question* (2006), University of Nebraska Press.

Kierna, Colm, 1931-2010, *Calwell* (1978), especially page 133.

Magness, Phillip and Sebastian Page, *Colonization After Emancipation: Lincoln and the Movement for Black Resettlement* (2011), University of Missouri Press. Stephen Dinan, 'Book: Lincoln sought to deport freed slaves,' *The Washington Times* newspaper, 9 February 2011. Robert Morgan, 'The 'Great Emancipator' and the Issue of Race – Abraham Lincoln's Program of Black Resettlement,' *Journal of Historical Review*, Volume 13, Number 5, September/October 1993. Dave Boyer and Susan Crabtree, 'Obama garbles U.S. history in human trafficking speech,' *The Washington Times* newspaper, 25 September 2012.

McCarthy, Eugene, 1916-2005, *A Colony of the World: The United States Today* (1992), Hippocrene Books, especially page 57.

Paine, Thomas, 1737-1809, *The Rights of Man* (1791-1792).

Putnam, Robert, born 1941, *Bowling Alone: The Collapse and Revival of*

American Community (2000), developed from his 1995 essay 'Bowling Alone: America's Declining Social Capital.'

Saunders, Doug, born 1967, *Arrival City: How the Largest Migration in History is Reshaping Our World*. Uncredited, 'City of cultures,' *The Sydney Morning Herald* newspaper, 23 December 2011.

Shaw, George Bernard, 1856-1950, *Back to Methuselah (A Metabiological Pentateuch)* (part 5, 1921).

Thomas, Gordon, born 1933, and Max Morgan-Witts, born 1931, *Voyage of the Damned* (1974). The film was released in 1976.

Films

2001: A Space Odyssey (1968), based upon the Arthur C Clarke story *The Sentinel* (1948).

2010 (1984), based upon the Arthur C Clarke novel *2010: Odyssey Two* (1982).

Life of Émile Zola, The (1937), based upon the Matthew Josephson, 1899-1978, biography *Zola and His Time* (1928).

Star Trek II: The Wrath of Khan (1982), written by Jack Sowards.

Star Trek III: The Search for Spock (1984), written by Harve Bennett.

Superman Returns (2006), written by Michael Dougherty and Dan Harris, directed by Bryan Singer.

X-Men (2000), written by David Hayter, directed by Bryan Singer.

Judgments and Tribunal Decisions

Inspector Ochoa v East Sun Building Pty Ltd and Gao (2010), New South Wales Industrial Relations Commission. Michael Tooma, 'Danger! Peligro! Publicity Order in Five Languages,' Norton Rose lawyers, 18 August 2011.

Mabo and Others v Queensland (No. 2) (1992) 175 CLR 1, [1992] HCA 23. Uncredited, 'Native Title changes flagged on Mabo anniversary,' *Australian Broadcasting Corporation News*, 4 June 2012.

MIMA v Naima Khawar [2002] HRD 18, (2002) 11(2) HRD 16, awarding a Pakistani woman allegedly suffering domestic violence refugee status. Janet Albrechtsen, 'Emotionalism triumphs over the law,' *The Australian* newspaper, 12 June 2002.

Minister for Immigration v Respondent 'A' and Respondent 'B'. On 16 June 1995, the Full Court of the Federal Court reversed Justice

Sackville's decision.

Parliamentary Reports

Hogg, Quintin McGarel, *Hansard*, Commons Sitting, Orders of the Day HC Deb 27 February 1968, Volume 759, cc1241-368 1241. Christian Joppke, born 1959, *Immigration and the Nation-State; The United States, Germany and Great Britain* (1999), Oxford University Press, page 110.

Reports

Australian Productivity Commission, *Economic Impacts of Immigration and Population Growth*, April 2006.

Camarota, Steven and Ashley Monique Webster, *Who Benefited from Job Growth In Texas? A Look at Employment Gains for Immigrants and the Native-Born, 2007 to 2011*, Centre for immigration Studies, 2011. Byron York, 'Study: Most new Texas jobs went to immigrants,' *Washington Examiner* newspaper, 22 September 2011.

Camarota, Steven and Karen Zeigler, *All Employment Growth Since 2000 Went to Immigrants*, Centre for immigration Studies, June 2014. Staff, 'Study: All Employment Growth Since 2000 Went to Immigrants,' *National Review Online*, 26 June 2014.

Fitzgerald, Stephen, *Immigration: A Commitment to Australia*, 1988. Richard Farmer, 'Will Labor have the immigration debate it squibbed in 1988?' *Crikey* website, 16 September 2010.

United Nations High Commissioner for Refugees, *Vietnamese refugees well settled in China, await citizenship*, 10 May 2007.

Songs

'I Write the Songs' (1975), written by Bruce Johnston and most famously sung by Barry Manilow.

'White Skin Black Heart' (1998), from the album *Redneck Wonderland*, by Midnight Oil.

Television Programmes

Current Affair, A (1988 onwards), Channel Nine, Australia, especially the segment titled 'All-Asian Malls' (7 November 2012). Uncredited, 'ACA 'All-Asian Mall' breached code: ACMA,' *Australian Associated Press* news service published at *News Limited Network*, 13 September 2013.

Dateline (1984 onwards), Special Broadcasting Service, especially 21 February 2012. Kirsty Needham, 'Biased, but refugee reviewer still has job,' *The Sydney Morning Herald* newspaper, 22 February 2012. Robert Birsel and Mirwais Harooni, 'Leaving migrants hurt Afghan economy,' *Australian Associated Press* news service published at *News Limited Network*, 11 December 2015.

Goodies, The (1970-1982). Nicola Fifield, 'Bill Oddie says large British families need to be 'contained',' *The Telegraph* newspaper, 19 October 2014.

Open Mind, The (1956 onwards). Richard Heffner interviewed Milton Friedman in the edition of 7 December 1975.

ABOUT THE AUTHOR

Simon Lennon has travelled throughout Europe, America, Australasia, Asia, and the South Pacific, seeing how similar European peoples are to each other (wherever we live) and how different we of the West are to everyone else. He has university bachelor's degrees in science and law and university master's degrees in commerce and business. He is married with six children.

His non-fiction collection *The West* comprises the following sixteen books:

Mending the West
The Unnatural West: An Overview
The Tribeless West: An Overview
The Homeless West: An Overview
The Vanishing West: An Overview

Individualism
Western Individualism
The End of Natural Selection
The Need for Nations

Identity
People's Identity: Race and Racism
Of Whom We're Born: Race and Family
Biological Us: Gender and Sexuality

Nationalism
A Land to Belong: Nationalism
The Failure of Multiculturalism

Cultures
Reclaiming Western Cultures
Christendom Lost
Aiding Islam

He is also the author of another non-fiction book, two collections of short stories, and five novels.

www.ingramcontent.com/pod-product-compliance
Lightning Source LLC
Chambersburg PA
CBHW020002290326
41935CB00007B/271